Quilt Small DREAM BIG

KARLA ALEXANDER

Unleash Your Creativity with Deceptively Simple Miniature Piecing

Why Can't We Be Friends, 62″ × 64″, by Karla Alexander, 2024

The center yin-yang symbol is composed of tiny Square in a Square blocks (page 24), often connected with bridges (page 28), slender wavy red sections join together, with occasional blocks and bridges adding interest to the background.

C&T PUBLISHING
Another Maker Inspired!

Publisher: Amy Barrett-Daffin

Creative Director: Gailen Runge

Senior Editor: Roxane Cerda

Technical Editor: Sarah Ruiz

Copy Editor: Second Glance Editorial

Cover/Book Designer: April Mostek

Production Coordinator: Zinnia Heinzmann

Illustrator: Aliza Shalit

Photography Coordinator: Rachel Ackley

Photography by C&T Publishing, Inc., unless otherwise noted

Published by C&T Publishing, Inc., P.O. Box 1456,
Lafayette, CA 94549

Library of Congress Cataloging-in-Publication Data

Names: Alexander, Karla, 1956- author

Title: Quilt small, dream big : unleash your creativity with deceptively simple miniature piecing / by Karla Alexander.

Description: Lafayette, CA : C&T Publishing, [2026] | Summary: "Unlock your stitching superpower! Learn to add miniature details that bring projects to life with clear guidance on fabrics, sewing, and personalization-then create five inspiring beginner projects to showcase your skills"-- Provided by publisher.

Identifiers: LCCN 2026007629 | ISBN 9781644036747 trade paperback | ISBN 9781644036754 ebook

Subjects: LCSH: Quilting | Patchwork | BISAC: CRAFTS & HOBBIES / Quilts & Quilting | CRAFTS & HOBBIES / Patchwork | LCGFT: Patterns (Instructional works)

Classification: LCC TT835 .A43495 2026 | DDC 746.46/041--dc23/eng/20260213

LC record available at https://lccn.loc.gov/2026007629

Printed in China

10 9 8 7 6 5 4 3 2 1

Little Stick Tree (page 53)

Acknowledgments

To my friends Lynn Bentson, Gaye Chimenti, and Janet Kok, who always see the potential in me as a teacher and quilt designer by continually fanning the sparks of my creativity into a healthy fire. They put their trust and confidence in me as I make my way through the ever-changing world of quilts. Their support has been the light I needed during the exciting and challenging process of writing this book. Thank you for your words of encouragement and for bringing out the best in me.

To my editor, Roxane Cerda, the first person I had contact with at C&T. Roxane showed me unwavering patience and compassion as I often changed my mind and started over again and again. Your ability to simplify the complex and smooth out the difficult is nothing short of amazing. Your constant reassurance helped me reach my full potential. I'm glad to have had you in my corner. Thank you for your commitment to my success; I couldn't have done it without your support.

Fabric postcard, 6½″ × 4½″

Contents

1. Courthouse Steps (page 72)
2. Improv Square in a Square (page 73)
3. Square in a Square (page 24)

PROJECTS 64

INTRODUCTION

Welcome to my world of patchwork! For as long as I can remember, I've been drawn to handmade things, both useful and decorative. Almost any patchwork, especially when created from an unusual grouping of fabric, continues to be a favorite of mine.

As a young girl, I was influenced by my mother, who frequently made utilitarian quilts for friends or family members to welcome a new baby into their home or celebrate a birthday, graduation, anniversary, or other important milestone. I got started making quilts by watching my mother. I loved tagging along to JCPenney, which had a fabric department on the basement floor. Arriving home, I would tear the fabric into squares and then pair them with other colors from the scrap box. I'd watch the pieces reunite in a field of patchwork, puff up with batting, and then later tighten up from the quilt stitches.

When I was older and moved away, my mother gifted me a sewing machine for my birthday. That's when I discovered a whole new world of quilting, flooded with colorful how-to books and a multitude of tools I could never have dreamed of. My mother's influence was contagious and to this day has enabled me to appreciate the satisfaction creativity provides.

Creating with fabric has been a continuous learning process for me. Understanding balance, pattern, and repetition has become a key element to my work. I'm self-taught and didn't major in any fine arts, although I often dream that one day, I might!

As I design, I prefer to work on a number of projects simultaneously, often using different methods for each. If boredom or frustration sets in, I find it's more productive for me to move on, keeping my focus fresh by shifting from one project to the next. Once I circle back, I'm usually able to tackle whatever I left behind with a new outlook.

My goal is to work toward **my** acceptable finish rather than completion, and I have three rules:

1 I don't settle. By that, I mean I do my best, stop as needed to work out any problems, and fix what needs to be fixed before moving on.

2 I set the bar at a reasonable place for me and stick to it. If something needs to be reworked and time is an issue, I set it aside and return to it when I have time to remedy the issue.

3 Although I enjoy reworking problem areas or pieces, I give myself permission to move on if something isn't calling to me.

If you are new to quiltmaking, I hope you'll find this book a useful addition to your growing creative toolbox. With these techniques, your skill level doesn't matter. Just browse the pages, determine a starting point that feels right for you, and go from there.

If you have more experience, just jump in and go for it. I hope you'll be inspired by the concepts and find new ideas to try out.

Enjoy!

WHAT ARE LITTLES?

Pincushion showcasing miniature elements, including spikes (page 33), a Square in a Square block (page 24), and a bridge outline (page 28)

Littles are tiny quilt elements, compositions, or blocks that inject that extra something into your patchwork. When they are added to projects, whether traditional or modern, improvisational or artistic, the results are amazing. My process, which I've named the *Reveal Method*, produces results that are as enjoyable as they are easy to achieve. The biggest difference with this piecing method is that you **sew first** *and then* **cut**. This method is the opposite of the usual piecing process, in which all the strips and squares are routinely precut to a particular size **and then** pieced together.

It takes only a little time to adapt to this method, and soon you'll be on your way. The Reveal Method is beneficial for those interested in learning an easy and innovative piecing technique that adds remarkable detail to your work and enhances your sewing skills along the way.

1

2

1. Detail of *Undercurrent*, 63″ × 82″, by Karla Alexander, 2023

   Little Log Cabin blocks (page 22), occasional bridges (page 28), and other Littles add visual interest to the quilt top.

2. Tiny spikes (page 33) with angled background piecing

Narrow bridges (page 28) add a lot of movement.

Bridges, narrow ¹⁄₁₆″–⅛″ strips, fuse fabrics together with an artistic flair or border elements as if drawn with paint pens. Tiny spikes are easy and fun to create and make great embellishments on everything quilty from handbags to greeting cards to place mats. Wine bags become impressive gifts on their own when a row of different colorful spikes is added around the perimeter. Tiny houses and trees are fun to make and become awesome wall hangings, postcards, or blocks to add to a pillowcase or quilt. The Reveal Method can also be used to downsize most traditional blocks, from 10″ or larger to as small as 2″–3″.

Once you learn this method, have fun and use it as a jumping-off point to discover your unique style and create work that previously seemed too difficult or time-consuming. I suggest trying out a few of the blocks and elements and then choosing a project. Give yourself permission to play as you go—exaggerate the widths or lengths of pieces or make each section more or less angled. You'll have a lot of fun while giving the usual process a boost of creativity.

Because Littles are so small, they don't need a lot of fabric and are a perfect way to use up leftovers. There is an undeniable satisfaction that results when creating something solely from your stash or leftover fabrics, and I'll bet you can relate. The projects and designs sprinkled throughout these pages are just waiting for you to take a look and give them a try. It's all within reach: Your imagination is the only limit. My hope is that you'll dive in and give Littles a try.

GETTING STARTED

Never fear—this book isn't based on any advanced sewing techniques, and you don't need to be a master quilter or piecer to be successful. Dive into these pages, and you'll learn how to modify and use a small ruler to reveal one fabric sliver at a time. Sewing a simple straight line with an accurate ¼″ seam allowance is the only skill you need to make this process productive, fun, and carefree.

When making Littles, you become the designer ... that is, *if you want to.* Think about any basic block you've made in the past and are comfortable with. Almost any can be "Little-ized," and the order of construction is usually identical to that of the full-size block. You can change the look by exaggerating the widths and lengths or by making sections thicker, thinner, or more angled.

Rail Fence framed quilt label

Good Vibrations fabric postcard, by Karla Alexander, 5¼″ × 7¼″, 2025

Littles can be used in so many places. Imagine using several itty-bitty Rail Fence blocks to build a border for a table runner, place mat, or even a wall hanging. Or, border a signed square or rectangle of fabric with tiny Rail Fence blocks creating a quilt label to give the perfect touch to a newly finished project. Littles can be used in cornerstones on quilt tops or incorporated into bags, table runners, or just about anything—there's almost always a spot where one will fit, enhancing your project.

One of my favorite things to do is to adhere a Little to card stock and make my own card with a small piece of fusible web or a glue stick. I promise, it will have a bigger impact than a purchased card, especially among quilter friends.

Materials and Tools

You don't need a lot to tackle Littles! In addition to your general quilting supplies, you'll want to gather the supplies listed below and then dive in:

- Small gridded quilt ruler*
- Snips or stiletto to help steer small pieces of fabric straight through the sewing machine
- Painter's tape in green or blue
- Painter's tape in a bright, contrasting color or a stack of 1″ × 1½″ sticky notes in bright colors
- Pad of paper and a pencil

Note:* Although any small square or rectangle ruler will work, I prefer a 2½″ × 6½″ ruler. This size works well when you're working with little pieces because it is easy to maneuver, and the slimmer width allows you to switch between the right and left sides with ease. If you can't find this size in your local quilt shop, you can purchase one from my website at **saginawstreetquilts.com

Check Your Seam Allowance

An accurate ¼″ seam allowance is crucial when sewing Littles. It's worthwhile to complete this simple check before beginning:

1 Cut a rectangle of fabric 1″ wider than it is long—for example, 7″ × 6″.

2 Position the rectangle with the short 6″ sides on the right and left and slice it vertically 2 times to create 3 strips. (It's okay if the strips are not exactly equal in width.)

3 Sew the 3 strips back together and press the seams open or to one side.

4 Place a square ruler on top of the block to measure the new dimensions.

- If it measures 6″ × 6″ square, the seam allowance is perfect.
- If it measures **less** than 6″ wide, the seam allowance is too wide. Adjust your seam allowance by moving the needle a tiny bit to the right, toward the raw edge of the fabric, to reduce the width.
- If it measures **more** than 6″ wide, the seam allowance is too scant. Adjust your seam allowance by moving the needle a tiny bit to the left, away from the raw edge of the fabric, to increase the width.

STEP 2

STEP 3

The Bungalow, 4″ × 5¼″, by Karla Alexander, 2025

Fabric Selection

Ideal Fabrics

For tiny piecing, I prefer 100% cotton fabric. In my opinion, it's the best choice and provides the best results. I usually don't prewash my fabric for Littles, but before cutting, I always press it with spray starch and a good amount of steam.

I choose my fabric for Littles entirely differently than I do for a typical patchwork quilt that often features medium to large prints. I do appreciate medium- and large-scale prints, but fabric for Littles needs to be cut into small sections so it can pass for a cloudy sky, tree branches, a river, or more.

To capture points and borders in a small patchwork project, the colors need to be distinctive from piece to piece. Solids, small-scale prints, and tone-on-tone fabrics that appear as a solid color from a distance (blenders) work best.

Townhouse Square postcard, 4″ × 6½″, by Karla Alexander, 2024

Consider how much surface area will be visible. If the pieces are narrow strips, the fabric will need to appear almost solid, without designs that might interrupt the flow of color. However, it's sometimes fun to find teeny-tiny prints or dots that will still show up in a ⅛″ strip. I'm always on the hunt for very small-scale prints.

If I have an area in my project where more than an inch will be visible, such as a border, I may consider a slightly larger pattern or design. A large print can completely change colors in a 2″ space and totally confuse the appearance. However, carefully placed, large prints can be perfect but may need a bit of fussy cutting. I cut a 1″ square out of an index card and use the window created as a viewing tool, sweeping it over a piece of fabric to "audition" small sections.

TIP

Littles require a minimal amount of fabric. Although that's a good thing, it's tricky to predict exact yardage, so raiding an existing stash can be handy. If you have a fabric stash, you more than likely have enough to try all the blocks in this book. If you need to purchase fabric, buy no more than a quarter yard or fat quarter. I rarely purchase more than that for Littles, and if I run out, I simply combine multiple pieces of the same color together with a bridge (page 28).

Just for fun, take a quick look at some of your less-desirable fabrics and picture them in several of the samples. I find I look at fabric differently when making Littles—pieces I didn't value before may be a perfect fit. It pays to study the lines and background shapes in a piece of fabric. Where before those designs may have been nearly unnoticeable, now they may be just what you need. When piecing siding for a house, branches for a tree, or other visual elements, you'll often find that these little shapes and lines end up working in your favor, doing a lot of the work for you. Stripes and polka dots can produce interesting results for skinny strips and bridges, appearing to be pre-pieced. You'll quickly realize a minimal amount of fabric is necessary to make a big impact. It's a great way to use up some of your leftover or less-favored fabrics.

Spider Web postcard, 5″ × 7″, by Karla Alexander, 2024

These highly patterned fabrics may look quite different when used for skinny strips and bridges.

Fabric Placement

It's extremely helpful to establish fabric placement before beginning to ensure that small points, squares, and border strips will be visible. The same goes when piecing several blocks for a border; do the pieces all need to match, or can they be scrappy? Once you've decided, you can move on to the next step.

For each project, I examine the block construction or design and determine what it needs to be successful. I find that it works well to look at my project and casually divide it into similar portions. Identify where you need light, medium, and/or dark values. Which part needs to stand out the most, and which portion can recede? Do I want high contrast or similar color values? Be aware of these factors and choose accordingly.

It's important to consider and audition high-contrast fabrics and those with similar values and colors. I prefer to assemble and choose from a group of fabrics that might work for one position rather than choosing just one piece, which creates more interest with the tiny pieces. After all, I have only a little space to make a big statement.

Pulse trivet, 7½″ × 7½″, by Karla Alexander, 2025
High contrast makes this Square in a Square pop.

Low contrast in color values causes pieces to blend.

Once I define my goal, I can continue making decisions. Look at a Log Cabin block, for example—I typically choose to have one side visually different from the other side and that the center needs to be different from either of those.

Avalon, 10″ × 10″, by Karla Alexander, 2025

Little Log Cabin blocks (page 22) pop in a two-color combination.

Or I may decide that the two sides of the block should be either contrasting fabrics or simply light and dark. Once I have reached this decision, I can begin assembling the fabrics for the different positions.

I depend a lot on what I call my *Ten-Foot Rule*. I place my fabric selections on a design wall because viewing horizontally can distort the view. (If a design wall isn't available, I use a light-colored sheet or large towel draped over the back of a couch or chair.) I ensure that an equal amount of each piece is showing. Once I have all my selections together, I step away approximately ten feet and then find a different color to quickly look at, such as the green grass or sky outside, before looking again at my selections.

Auditioning fabrics from a distance makes it easy to determine when pieces need to be removed or added, helping me enjoy the process. I continue adding and removing pieces until I'm satisfied. I then take a few pictures, walk away, and look at my selections as seen on camera for a different view. Using these methods, it becomes obvious when a fabric isn't working. Sometimes, fabrics might be too close in value or might stand out too much, which is easier to tell from farther away.

Colors can be enhanced or weakened, depending on what they are combined with. With Littles, this trait becomes even more apparent—a color that seemed bright in your fabric collection might seem dull next to another color when placed on a design wall in good light. You don't need to be a color guru to know what you do and don't like, especially once you get used to using a design wall and taking your time to make decisions. Experiment with color combinations, add unexpected pieces, and take snapshots along the way. I hope you'll give my Ten-Foot Rule a try to see whether it works for you.

TIP

If you'd like to study the science and art of using the color wheel efficiently as well as how colors relate to one another, an unlimited amount of information on color theory is available in books and on the internet.

KICK OUTS

I suggest using scrap or leftover fabrics when trying out a new block or making a sample. I do my best to add only fabric I like or love to my stash, but if I repeatedly bypass a fabric for one reason or another, I'll pluck it out and keep it in a different area I refer to as the "kick outs." When working on a new sample, I use the kick outs to see how the block sews up. After making my sample, I use a pen to write any necessary notes right on the completed block. This method provides a record for me, noting what needs to be corrected as well as what works. After I've worked out the bugs, I go through my stash and choose a combination for my new block.

Once I'm satisfied with my selections, if one of my choices is from a large piece of fabric, I trim a 3″–4″ strip off the shortest edge. I leave smaller pieces as they are and trim them to size as I go. Although it is occasionally necessary to precut a piece of fabric to a specific size or shape—for example, the center square in a Log Cabin block—I usually trim off chunks or strips of fabric as I sew.

THE REVEAL METHOD

Your Reveal Ruler

Littles are achieved by using a small ruler as a window to reveal narrow strips and sections. I recommend using a 2½″ × 6½″ gridded acrylic ruler. A small ruler works well when working with small pieces because it's easy to maneuver without any unnecessary length getting in the way. It's also the perfect width, as you'll often use the right and left sides simultaneously. The instructions below assume you're working with a 2½″ × 6½″ ruler, but if you're unable to find this size at your local quilt shop, you can purchase one from my website at **saginawstreetquilts.com** or grab any small square or rectangular quilting ruler.

To make your Reveal Ruler:

1 Gather a small gridded acrylic ruler and painter's tape.

2 Peel off a piece of tape slightly longer than the ruler. Perfectly align the tape with the ¼″ measurement along the length of the ruler. Press the tape down in place covering the ¼″ width along the edge.

3 Use a rotary cutter or craft knife to trim the excess tape even with the edges of the ruler.

4 *Optional:* I apply brightly colored painter's tape or sticky notes along the opposite long edge, exactly as I applied the painter's tape to the first edge. This technique is handy when working with blue and purple fabrics because it can sometimes be difficult to distinguish between the tape and the fabric. Following this step gives you different colors on either side of the ruler so you can flip back and forth, depending on whether you are cutting light or dark fabric.

STEP 3

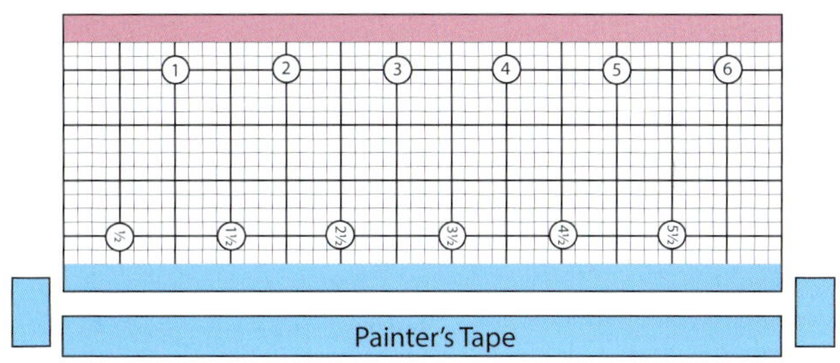

STEP 4

Using Your Reveal Ruler

Now that you've made your Reveal Ruler, it's time to take it for a test drive. In a nutshell, your modified ruler allows you to preview a narrow slice of fabric by revealing its width so you are able to see exactly what will show in your finished piece. The masked edge of the ruler covers and provides the exact ¼″ seam allowance you'll need. Remember that the covered ¼″ will be hidden in the seam allowance.

Remember, unlike most quilting projects, with Littles, you **sew and then cut** rather than first cutting out all the pieces and then sewing them together. Even though you are working in miniature, don't trim your seam allowances; they will fall into place as you go, with minimal bulk.

For tiny piecing, I find that finger-pressing is just as effective as using an iron, and often easier to do. Just remember to wash your hands before you begin to remove any oils or lotions that could transfer to your work. For larger pieces or complete blocks, I use an iron for pressing.

To try the Reveal Method, follow the steps below, sewing pieces together and then trimming to size as directed. This process is likely backward from what you're used to.

1 Cut 3 rectangles, 1 light and 2 dark, each approximately 1½″ × 3½″.

2 Sew a light and dark rectangle together, right sides together (RST), and finger-press the seam toward the dark fabric.

3 Place the combined pieces right side up, with the dark rectangle on the left and the light piece on the right. Place the ruler on top of the combined strips, **aligning the inner edge of the tape along the seam**. Slide the ruler slightly to the right, revealing ¼″ of the light fabric **between the seam and the inner edge of the tape**: This is your window. For a narrower strip, slide the ruler back toward the left, revealing only ⅛″ of light fabric. The tape obscures the ¼″ strip of fabric that becomes the seam allowance.

4 Once you have fine-tuned the width of the fabric in your window and are satisfied with the result, cut along the outer edge of the ruler.

STEP 2

STEP 4

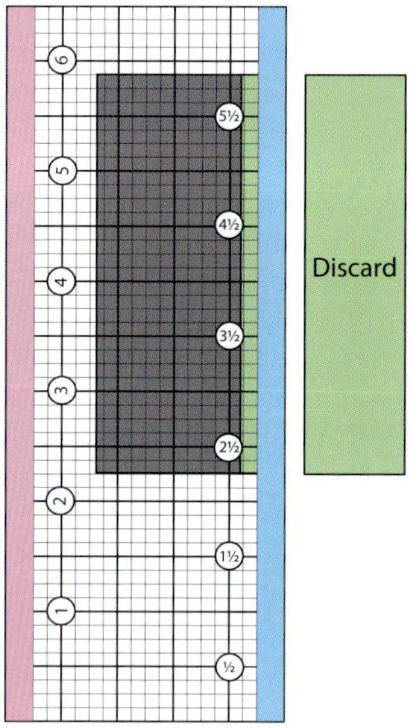

The Reveal Ruler shows approximately ⅛″ of light fabric. This thin strip is what will show in the finished piece.

STEP 5

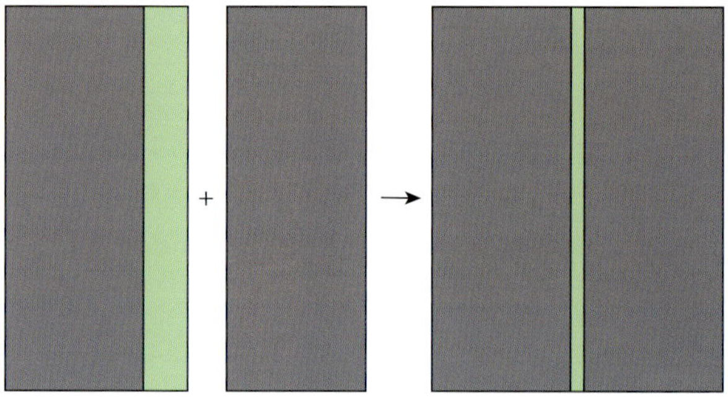

5 Add the second dark strip, RST, along the trimmed edge and press the seam toward the dark fabric. This step completes the reveal.

Although I listed a starting size in Step 1, when working on an actual project, simply choose your fabric and cut oversized pieces. You can also estimate the finished size of a particular piece and then add about an inch to each dimension. The excess will be trimmed off as you work.

Determining Piecing Order

When using the Reveal Method, work in the same piecing order as you would if you were making the block traditionally. If you are not familiar with the traditional piecing order for a block or you are making an improv block, you can determine the piecing order by using what I call the *through line*. A through line is a line that extends from one edge of the block across to the opposite edge.

In a Log Cabin block, for example, it's clear that a square is in the center of the block. However, to separate the block piece by piece, you must start with the longest outside edge first, following the through line.

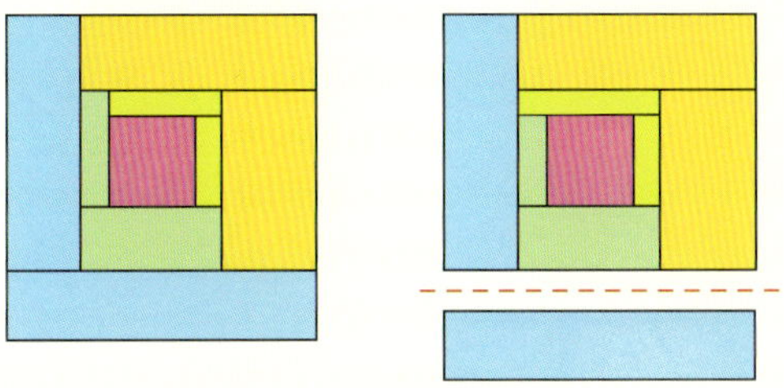

Gravity, 10½″ × 13″, by Karla Alexander, 2025

You then continue around the block, pulling off the next longest piece until you reach the center square. Your piecing order will be the reverse of how you deconstructed the block. By making a quick drawing of a block, I can find the through line, which will always be the starting point.

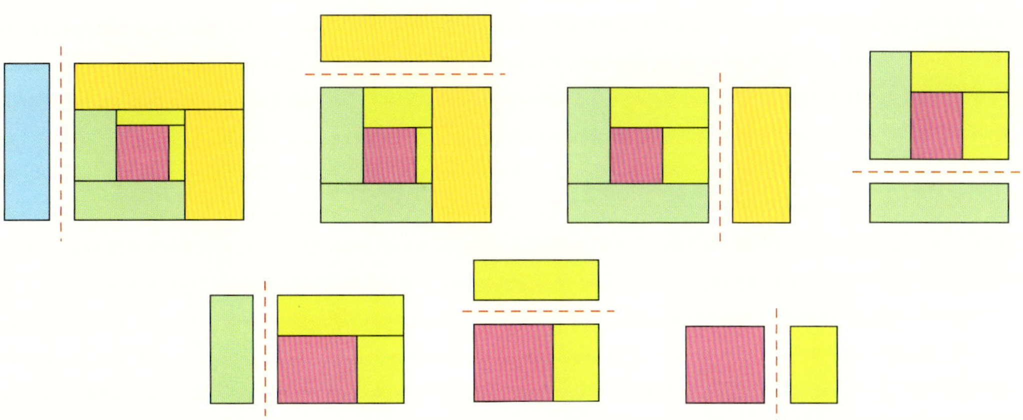

TIP

When using the Reveal Method, work in the same piecing order as you would if you were making the block traditionally. The first piece can be roughly pretrimmed to a particular shape or size as desired, but don't forget to add extra width and length to account for the seam allowance.

Next, look at a simple House block. It's clear that some sections need to be pieced together first before combining them to form other pieces. Locate the first through line by finding a seam that travels from the left side of the house all the way to the right side of the house. Separating on the through line means you can slide the roof section up and away from the block. For the roof section, look for the through lines. In this case, all lines are through lines, so work from the center out.

The next through lines traveling from edge to edge, separating sections, are the ground section and the bridge.

That leaves the middle house section. The two sections on the right of the door have seams that travel from the top to bottom edge of the house.

The next through line is the left section of the house, leaving the door unit. The seam line runs vertically from top to bottom.

The last piece is the door and the overhead piece of the house. The seam line runs horizontally through from edge to edge. Now that the block is deconstructed, it's easy to see where to start; construct the block by working in the opposite order, building the door section, then adding the house front sections, and then continuing in reverse order.

Once you're familiar with the Reveal Method and how to deconstruct a block by finding through lines, you are ready to dive in and make your own Littles. Choose a block and make a rough sketch, with the pieces numbered for order of assembly. If you are familiar with the piecing order, this step isn't necessary, but if you are trying out a new block, I think you'll find it useful. Your sketch doesn't need to be perfect—no one else will see it!

Now that you have your piecing order and your fabric choices, get your fabric ready to go. There's no precutting numerous strip sets and shapes; simply rough cut chunks or strips a few inches larger than you think you'll need for each section. Stack your fabrics in the order you'll use them. Let's dive in!

BASIC BLOCKS

Undercurrent, 63″ × 82″, by Karla Alexander, 2023

Little Log Cabin

Use your Reveal Ruler when piecing a Log Cabin block to make it easy to adjust the width of the *logs* (strips). Select your fabric and lay the pieces out in order, so they are handy. I often begin with a piece approximately 1″ square for the center.

When making a Log Cabin block, add the pieces in a circular manner, beginning in the center and then continuing by adding a piece to the left, bottom, right, and then top. Add your first piece to the left of the center. Snip off any excess that hangs past the edge of your piece.

Now, the fun begins: Use your Reveal Ruler to determine how much of the just-added piece you want to show and then trim off the excess. (You'll want to rotate the patchwork each time you add a piece to make trimming easy.)

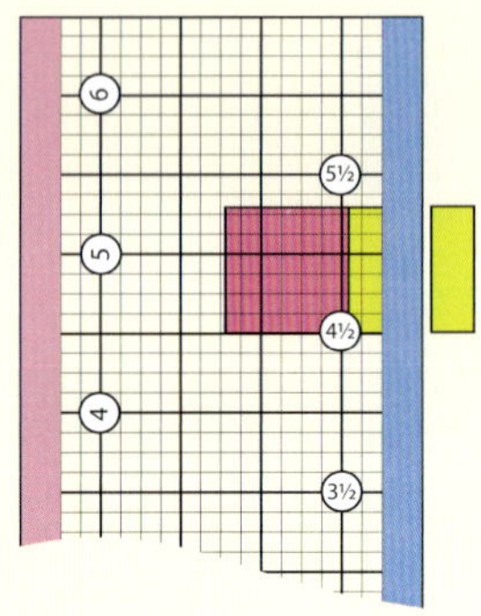

Add the next piece. Continue to add pieces in a circular manner until you have achieved the desired block size.

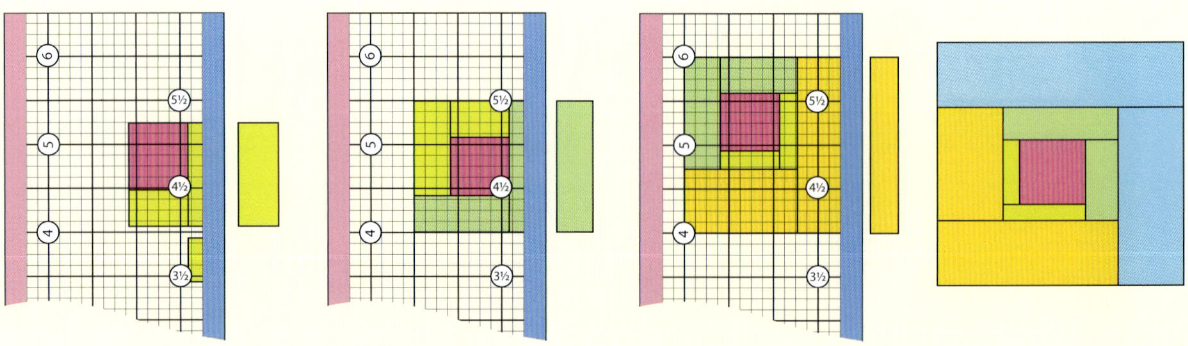

Once you have the traditional Log Cabin down, there are several variations to try! I choose the style depending on my project. Sometimes, I prefer the logs to all be equal in width, while other times, I like them to look more playful by adjusting the width or angle of the logs. You could even try piecing a Log Cabin with logs added in a nontraditional fashion, pieced around the center in random order, sometimes adding two pieces on one side before moving on. It's so much fun to make these little blocks, and there are so many places they will fit.

Log Cabin with unevenly sized logs

Log Cabin with angled logs

Log Cabin with random piecing

The center square can be as big or as small as you'd like. Sometimes, a large center square with tiny logs provides a big impact, and using tiny logs on one side and wide ones on the other gives a completely different look. With different sized logs on either side, the center square will always be off-center.

Large center with tiny logs

Large center with tiny logs
on one side, wider on the other

Little Square in a Square

Using a Reveal Ruler when piecing a Square in a Square block makes it easy to adjust the width of the logs. This block is similar to a Log Cabin in that you begin in the center of the block and work outward, but for this block, you work side to side and then up and down rather than in a circular fashion. Adjusting the width or angling the logs results in a variety of styles. The center piece can be small or large, and the logs around it can be angled, all the same width, or each different.

Square in a Square with angled logs

Square in a Square with varying width logs

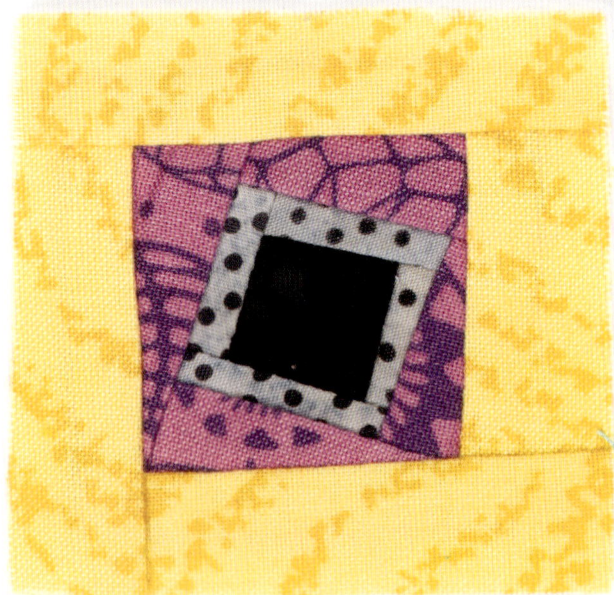

Square in a Square combining straight and angled logs

Little Spiral

Just as with the Log Cabin and Square in a Square, a Spiral block has piecing that works around a center, and using a Reveal Ruler makes it easy to adjust the width of the strips (logs) to achieve a variety of looks. The logs can all be the same width, a variety of widths, or even angled.

The piecing order for this block is a little trickier, but once you know the order, it's easy. You can choose to piece in a clockwise or counterclockwise order.

To piece a Spiral block, I use the piecing order outlined below. I keep a little chart next to me while I sew to help stay in order.

TIP

If the Spiral block appeals to you, download a copy of this chart and keep it handy! To access the chart through the tiny URL, type the web address provided into your browser window.

tinyurl.com/11648-patterns-download

TIP

After the first, second, and third logs have been added to the center, each subsequent log will be sewn over the top of two seams. This edge will be the only one that has two seams, so you can always determine which side is next.

Light Center

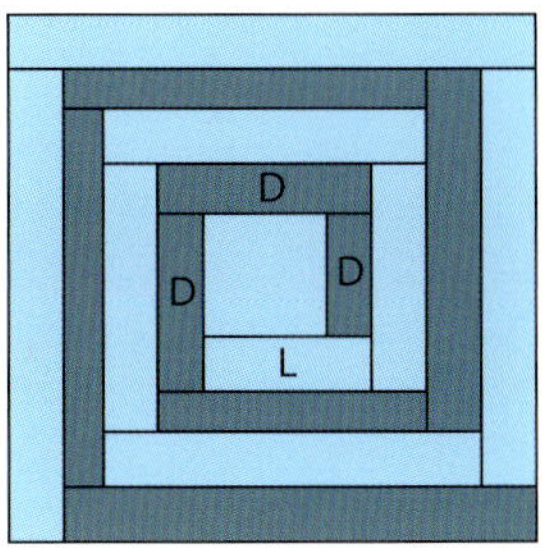

When starting with a light center, add pieces in this order: dark, light, dark, dark; then light, dark, light, light. Repeat the sequence until you have the number of rounds you'd like.

LIGHT CENTER

Repeat this sequence for as many rounds as desired.

Round One	D	L	D	D
Round Two	L	D	L	L

The letter "D" refers to a dark piece, and the letter "L" refers to a light piece.

Dark Center

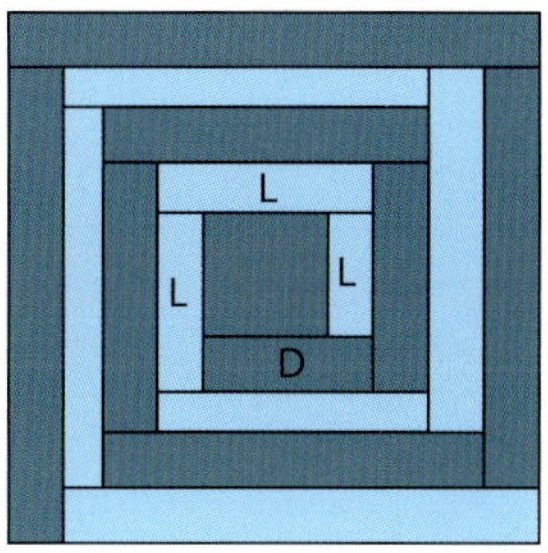

When starting with a dark center, add pieces in this order: light, dark, light, light; then dark, light, dark, dark. Repeat the sequence until you have the number of rounds you'd like.

DARK CENTER

Repeat this sequence for as many rounds as desired.

Round One	L	D	L	L
Round Two	D	L	D	D

The letter "D" refers to a dark piece, and the letter "L" refers to a light piece.

Angled

To add a little spice to your spiral, you can angle the logs, vary the widths, or even change the color of the center square. You could also consider piecing a spiral around an existing or leftover block.

Passages, 7″ × 7″, by Karla Alexander, 2025
Uneven logs, some with additional piecework

Little Spiral block with angled logs

Little Spiral block with bridges (page 24)

FUSSY CUTTING

Any block that begins with a center square is a perfect opportunity to showcase a bit of fussy cutting. Simply isolate a small motif in your fabric and use your Reveal Ruler to cut it to size so you automatically account for the seam allowance. Depending on the block you choose, you can create a simple frame or make it the centerpiece of a more complex block. Using blocks that reveal a tiny motif can create a fun effect in a finished piece, such as in the Love postcard (page 75).

Downsize Almost Any Block

You can turn any block into a Little as long as that block has straight lines. The easiest blocks to reduce in size are blocks that begin with a center or one edge because those blocks tend to have fewer overlapping seam allowances.

If you'd like to downsize a particular block, grab a piece of paper and make a quick sketch. Refer back to Determining Piecing Order (page 19) to deconstruct the block, pick your fabrics, and you're on your way.

As far as the finished size goes, you could calculate the widths and lengths, but I simply begin smaller or larger, depending on the need.

Off Grid, 8″ × 10″, by Karla Alexander, 2025

BRIDGES

River Runs Through It, 21″ × 41″, by Karla Alexander, 2023

Bridges are tiny slices of fabric, ⅟16″–¼″ wide, that are used to add a pop of color to a block or border or to join fabrics in a creative way. When working on projects like the ones in this book, I take advantage of each seam and determine whether it is a good place to build a bridge.

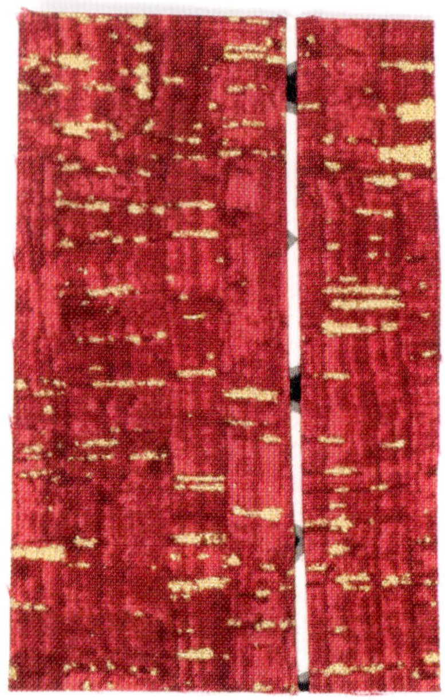

⅛″ (top) and ⅟16″ (bottom) bridges

When I've run out of fabric for a border, block, or backing, I am left either trying to find more of that particular fabric or matching it with a similar piece I have on hand. Choosing an alternate fabric is an opportunity to add a bridge. I find that this tiny slice of fabric adds more visual interest than a simple seam, which may look like a mistake, especially with a slight change in the fabric color.

Also, when preparing a larger background piece to use for insetting circles or other piecework, I like to use several similar pieces joined with bridges, as I feel it creates more interest.

Nexus, 18½″ × 60″,
by Karla Alexander, 2024

Tilt trivet, 7″ × 7″, by Karla Alexander, 2024

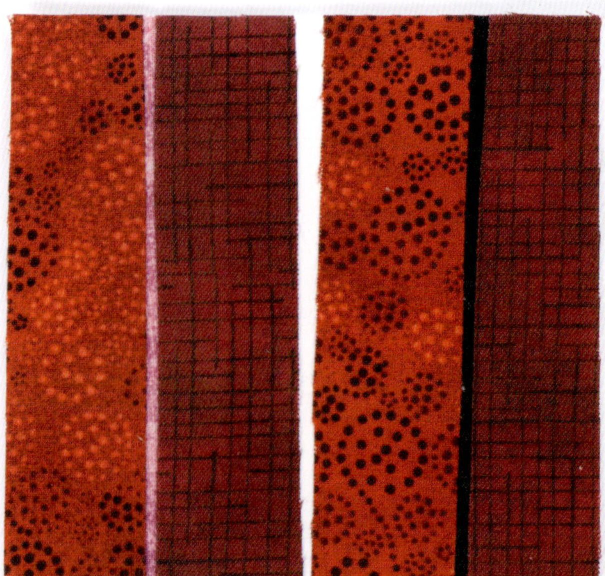

Sometimes, I add a bridge just for fun. I often use multiple pieces of the same or similar colors joined with a bridge for the same position in a block rather than just one fabric piece. After all … I have just a little space to make a big statement.

Choose the background fabric(s) and the bridge fabric. Because bridges are so tiny, it's crucial to choose a fabric with a high-contrast value or color compared to the background pieces; otherwise, the bridge will disappear. In the exercise on the next page, I indicate sizes for the background pieces, but in your project, they may be any size at all, although bridge fabric strips need to be only about 1″ wide.

Bridge construction is a perfect example of when you must use a straight, accurate ¼″ seam allowance. A wiggly or wayward seam will distort the bridge, often making it disappear altogether (see Check Your Seam Allowance, page 10).

Follow the steps below to make a sample bridge.

1 For the background, cut a strip of medium to dark value fabric approximately 3″ × 5″. For the bridge, cut a strip of contrasting fabric approximately 1½″ × 5″.

2 Vertically slice the background fabric in half, yielding 2 strips 1½″ × 5″ each.

3 Using an accurate ¼″ seam allowance, sew the 1½″ bridge strip to a background piece.

4 Finger-press or use an iron to press the seam allowance toward the background strip.

5 Place the combined piece on a cutting mat, with the short edges positioned at the top and bottom and the bridge piece on the right. (If you cut left-handed, position it with the bridge piece on the left.) Place the Reveal Ruler on top, aligning the tape line with the seam. Rotate your ruler so that the highest contrast tape is overlapping the revealed fabric.

6 To reveal a 1/16″ slice of bridge fabric, slide the ruler away from the background a tiny bit. The tape is hiding the seam allowance, so what you see is the actual width the bridge will be once the strip set is cut and sewn to the remaining background piece.

To experiment with the width of the bridge, slide the ruler farther away from the background fabric.

STEP 2

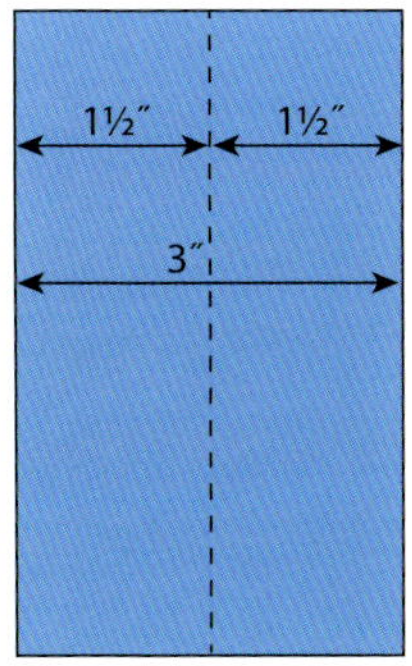

STEP 3

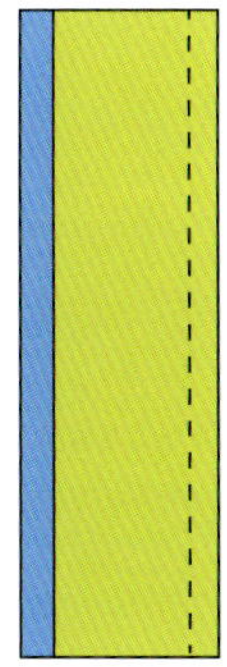

STEP 4

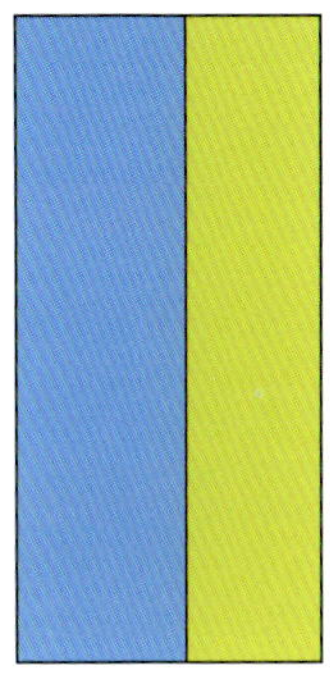

STEP 5

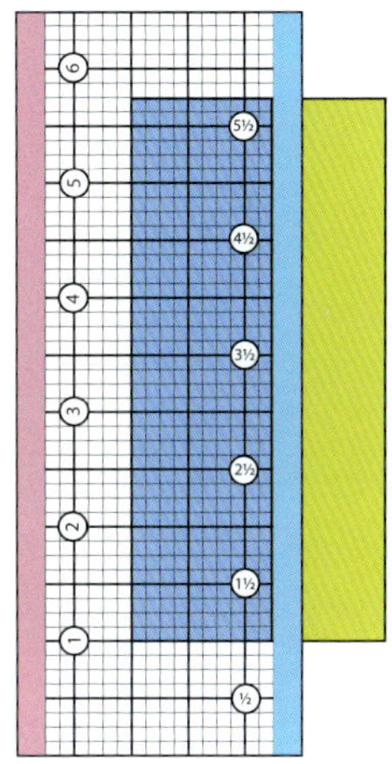

STEP 6

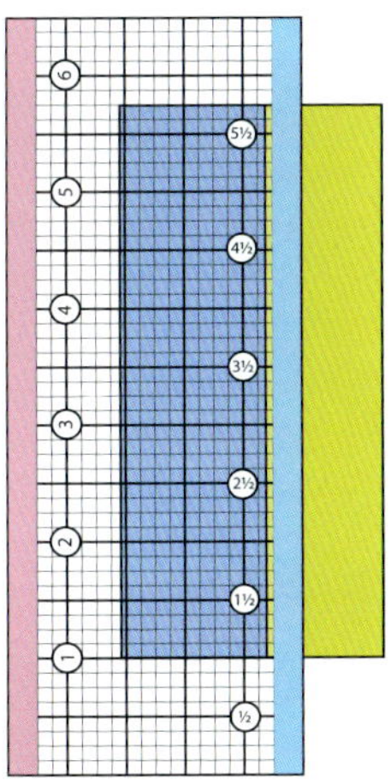

Reveal 1/16″.

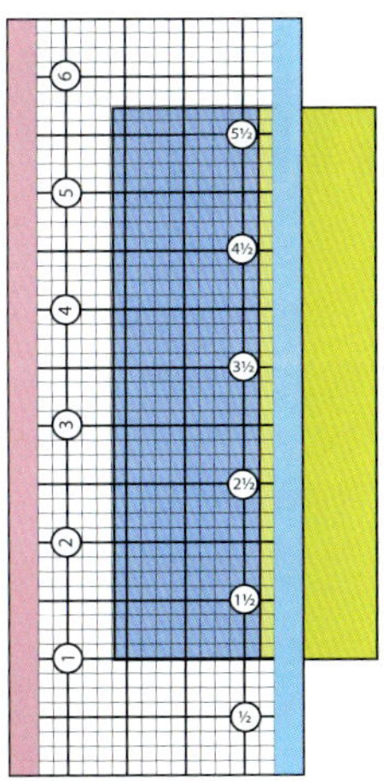

Reveal 1/8″.

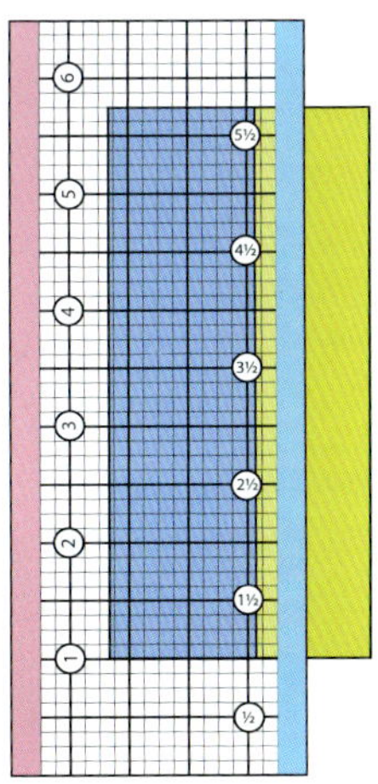

Reveal 3/16″.

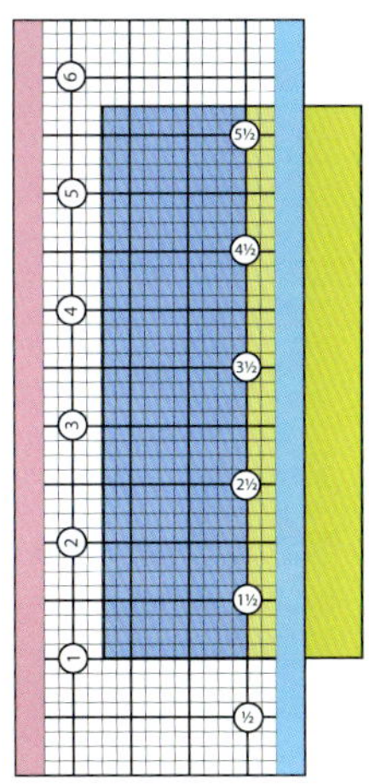

Reveal ¼″.

7 Once you've chosen your bridge width, cut along the edge of the ruler. Discard the excess bridge fabric.

8 With right sides together, sew the pieced unit to the remaining background piece. I prefer to sew with the pieced unit on the bottom, as it seems to stay in place better; however, by putting the pieced unit on top, you'll be able to see the first seam, which might help you guide your new piece through the sewing machine, viewing the bridge width as you sew. Either way works, as long as you maintain an accurate ¼″ seam allowance. Press the seam toward the new background piece.

STEP 8

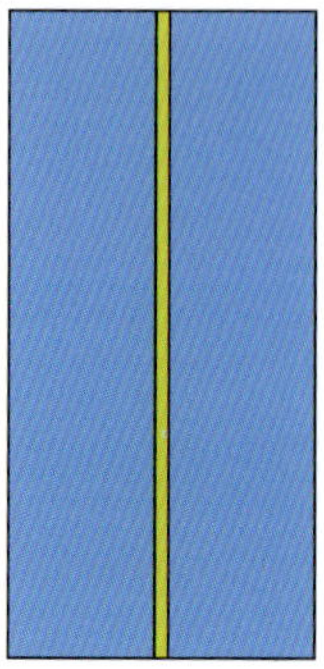

Once you are comfortable constructing bridges, have a little fun and experiment with bridge widths and fabric choices. Use a small- to medium-scale print for an interesting bridge effect. A favorite choice of mine is to use fabric with stripes, which often looks like I have pieced tiny strips in the bridge fabric.

TIP

For an even more interesting look, you can construct a pieced strip and then use that strip to create a bridge that contains piecing!

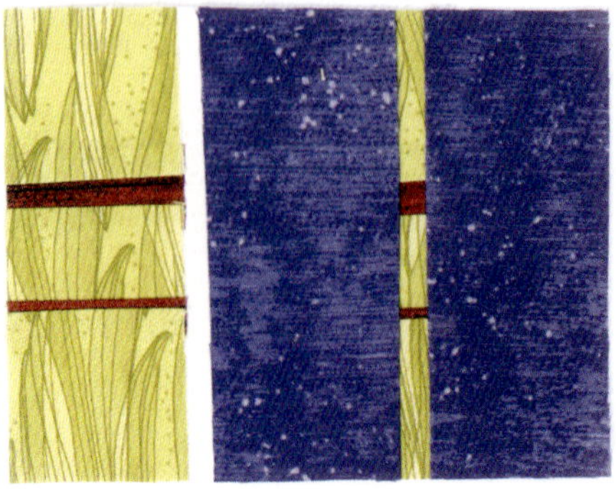

SPIKES

Spikes are another creative way to add a little excitement to your quilt projects, and they are easy to make in a variety of sizes. I love making them and am always drawn to their hand-cut organic look; each one is a little different from the next, without requiring the use of a specialty ruler or template.

Improv New York Beauty, 52″ × 73″, by Karla Alexander, 2023

Spikes work really well:

- Around the corner border of a quilt (one of my favorite places to use them!)
- As an accent for small projects, such as totes or wine bags
- Paired with inset circles

They are especially awesome when randomly bordering blocks.

When making spikes, I prefer to use a lot of different fabrics, although they will turn out just fine when made with two fabrics, one for the spikes and another for the background. Be sure that your background and spike fabric contrast so that the spike, or a portion of it, doesn't get lost.

The point gets lost because the values of the dark pink and black are too similar.

Once I began using spikes in my work, I quickly realized how easy they were to alter. You can make short spikes, skinny spikes, tall narrow spikes, tiny spikes, pieced spikes—as many different spikes as you can imagine. Regardless of which you choose to try, make sure to use your Reveal Ruler to determine the size and shape of the spike.

Single Spikes

Individual spikes are fun and easy to make. With this method, you can stack them atop one another to create a vertical strip, use them individually, or use them any way you wish.

1 Decide how tall you'd like the spike to be and cut rectangles ½″–¾″ wider than they are tall. You'll need 1 spike and 1 contrasting or background rectangle; these 2 rectangles will make 2 blocks.

Love postcard, 6¼″ × 4½″, by Karla Alexander, 2025

2 Layer the 2 rectangles right sides up, with the short edges on the right and left. Draw a line ½″ from the top edge. Use your Reveal Ruler to cut an angle on the right side of the rectangle, as wide or skinny as you wish. Slide the cut-away corner piece out of the way and then cut the left angle, crossing over the cut at the top so the point of the spike is on the line or, at a minimum, ¼″ from the top edge.

STEP 2

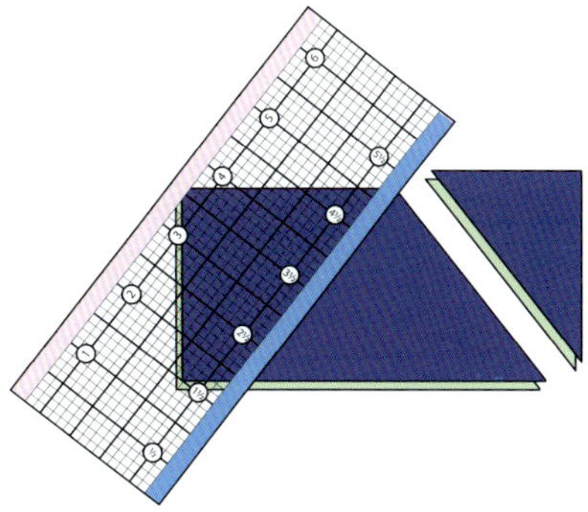

TIP

If you are making more than two spikes at a time, start with that number of rectangles; four rectangles will make four spikes, etc. In Step 2, alternate contrasting colors in your stack before cutting. After cutting, shuffle the top layer of the center spike stack to the bottom of the stack. If you layered multiple colors, also shuffle down two pieces from either the right or left, resulting in a different color on each side of the spike.

For an added spark, you can make multiple stacks and mark the center points off-center so your spikes aren't identical. Or, when marking the center points, incrementally position the points of subsequent stacks slightly to the right and then back toward the left. When piecing is complete, the spikes will appear to swerve right and back to the left.

STEP 3

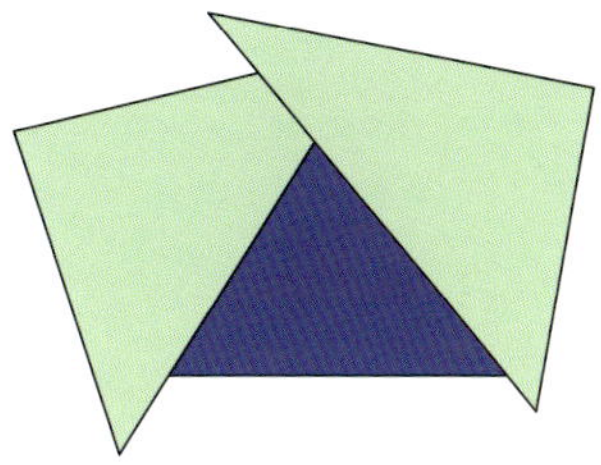

3 Pair a center spike with 2 background pieces, stitch them together, and press the seams to the side.

4 To trim the top edge straight, rotate the spike so the point is positioned to the right. Use your ruler and align the inner edge of the tape with the point on the spike; keep the ruler straight and aligned with the sides of the block and trim away the excess. Trimming in this manner prevents you from accidentally chopping off the tip!

STEP 4

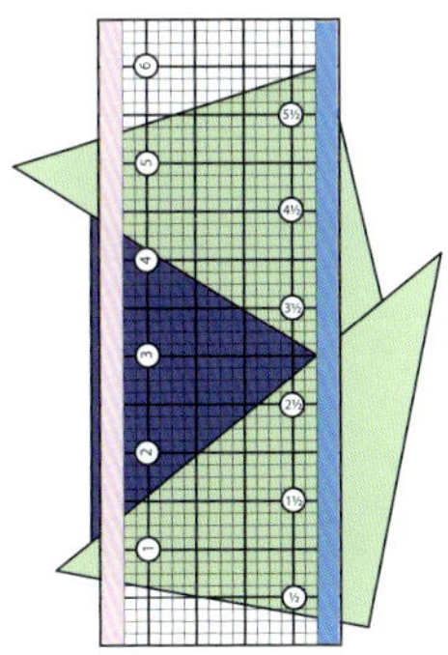

5 Trim the sides and bottom to the desired size. It's fine to have a little extra background showing on the right and left sides, but be sure that the side seam is within ¼″ of the lower corner or that the cut shoots right through the corner. If it's more than a ¼″ away from the corner, the finished spike will look square on the bottom.

STEP 5

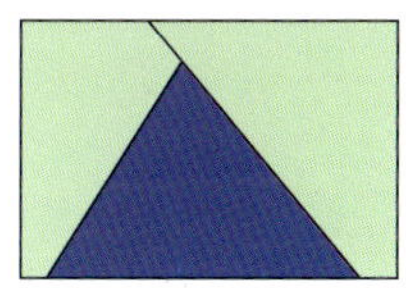

Spikes in a Row

You can also make a row of spikes, which are a nice design element when bordering a block. It's easy to change the size by starting with larger or smaller pieces of fabric. Gather some scraps and dive in!

You can piece rows together or use them individually. If you need an exact length, consider making the spikes wider or narrower, depending on what you need. Also, leave a wider space at the beginning and end of each strip if length is an issue; the added length will allow you to piece the strips together.

1 Choose 2 contrasting colors, one for the spikes and one for the background. I like to choose a variety of fabrics for each color, such as 3 similar blues and 3 similar golds.

2 To make a row of spikes 3″–4″ tall, cut 3 rectangles 5″ × 13″ for the background and 3 rectangles 5″ × 13″ for the spikes. This will create 6 spike strips: 3 with your intended spike fabric and 3 with the spike fabric as the background fabric.

TIP

For row spikes, I suggest beginning with 13″–20″ lengths. If you have fat quarters, I find it easy to trim strips from the short 18″ end. The longer the strip, the more spikes you can make.

3 Layer the strips right sides up in a stack with edges aligned, alternating the 2 colors; it doesn't matter which color is first. Use a chalk marker or fabric marker to make a horizontal line ½″ from the top and bottom edges. Draw the spikes, making the bottoms 3½″–4″ wide; the tip should always land at the horizontal line. Center the top point or nudge it a bit off-center so they aren't all identical. If you are right-handed, I suggest that you begin drawing the spikes from the right side (and vice versa if you are left-handed) to ensure your pieces fit together naturally.

4 Cut your spikes. Each time you cut a spike, be aware that the second cut will trim off a portion of the excess on the next spike, outside the ½″ line. This outcome is correct and will make it easier to align the pieces.

5 Shuffle the pieces. Referring to the illustration, peel off the number of layers noted, and place them on the bottom of that stack.

TIP

Before piecing, I like to pin the spikes in order to a piece of paper or fabric. This step keeps them in order in case I accidentally drop a stack or two!

6 Begin piecing with the first spike on the left. Offset the tips and background pieces to make sure that the top edge is aligned and that the spikes are always at least ¼″ from the top edge. Sew the pieces together and then press the seam away from the new piece. Continue to add pieces to complete the strip.

TIP

To chain piece the spikes, sew together the pieces in the first two stacks, one layer at a time. Next, bring the beginning of the chain back toward yourself, finger-press the previous seam away from the new piece, and then add the first piece in the third stack. Continue in this manner, adding one stack at a time, until all the stacks have been added.

7 When the strip is complete, use a long ruler to trim the top and bottom edges straight, making sure to leave at least ¼″ between each point and the edge (top and bottom). If you want to piece the rows together, trim them all to the same height. Layer the short ends of 2 strips, making sure that the color order is correct. Lay your ruler across the join, angling it until you like the look of the new spike, and then trim along the edge. This step will automatically cut the bottom piece as well so they can be pieced together. Piece all the rows together or leave them in sections, as desired.

STEP 4

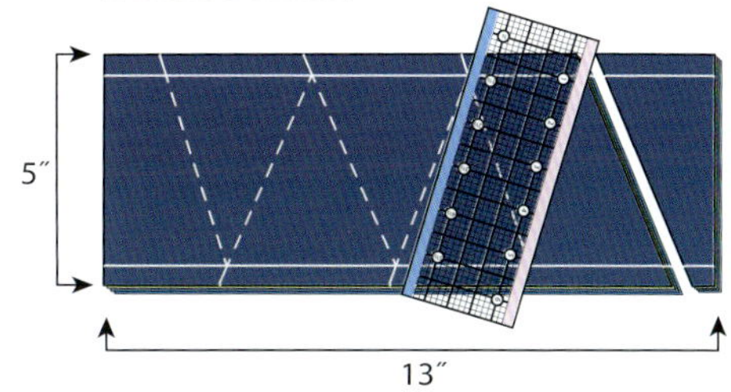

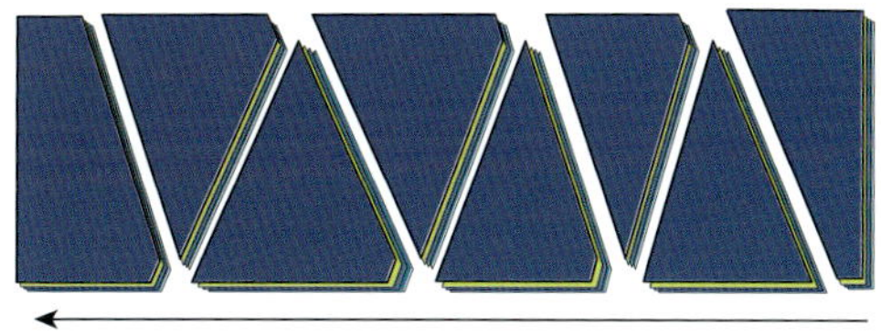

Cut from right to left.

STEP 5

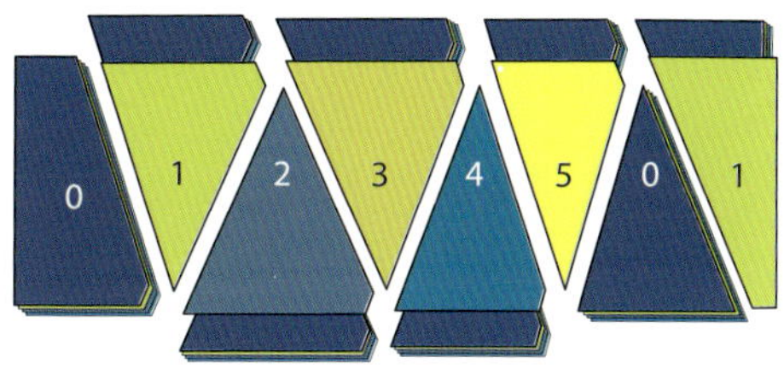

STEP 6

STEP 7

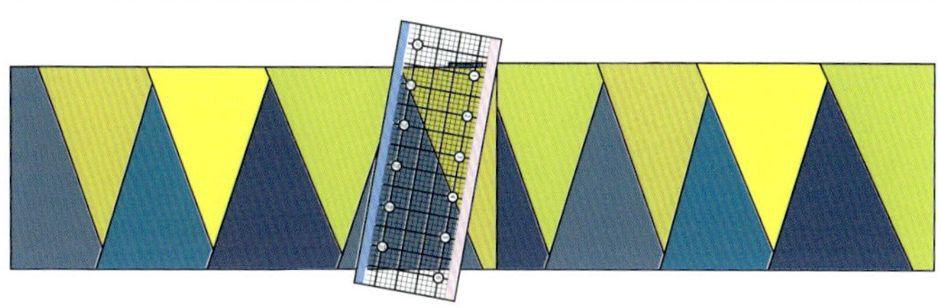

TIP

If any strips are significantly shorter than the others, consider adding a narrow background strip to the top or bottom as an additional embellishment and making a bridge to add that extra piece.

HOUSES AND NEIGHBORHOODS

Simple Houses

Little houses are so much fun to make, and once you start, it's hard to stop. I think you'll see fabric in a whole new way when working at this small scale, especially with houses and trees. Fabrics you may not have liked will now have a different appeal. A lot of tone-on-tone and small-scale prints work great for houses. Sometimes, even a large print can make a great tree or roof when cut into smaller pieces. Look at the fabric used in some of the book samples to see how tiny stripes, crooked lines, and dots can bring life to a window, house siding, or grass and trees. When you are ready to piece a little house, I suggest starting with a simple house, meaning no chimney, doors, or windows. I love this design for its simplicity and used it for my *Simple Neighborhood* table runner (page 40).

1 To begin, sketch a simple house on paper. You don't need to worry, no one will see it except you. Add the background behind the rooftop.

2 Separate the pieces of your drawing, and then it's time to choose the fabric. As with most Littles, small-scale prints or solids often work best. As always, roughly precut your fabric selections and keep them handy.

3 The sketch will help you determine the piecing order (see Determining Piecing Order, page 19).

4 Using your sketch as a reference, cut your chosen fabrics into rough rectangles or square pieces a bit larger than the pieces you've sketched. When in doubt, cutting larger is the rule! More mistakes happen when you're trying to use pieces that are too small.

5 Trim the roof piece into a rectangle and then trim the ends off at approximately 45° angles. The angle doesn't need to be perfect; try not to overthink this part.

6 Cut 1 background square and 1 house square (for the gable) in half diagonally.

7 Sew the pieces for the roof section together, making sure to leave ¼″ between the top tip of the gable and the top edge and ¼″ on the left side of the gable to allow for the seam allowance when adding the background. Finger-press or iron the seams in one direction. Set aside.

8 For the bottom part of the house, sew the pieces you chose for the front and side sections together and then press the seam in the opposite direction of the seam at the gable.

9 Sew the 2 sections together, making sure to leave ¼″ from the roof corners to the side of the block so that the corners of your roof do not disappear into the seam allowance. Finger-press or iron the seam toward the bottom portion of the house.

STEP 1

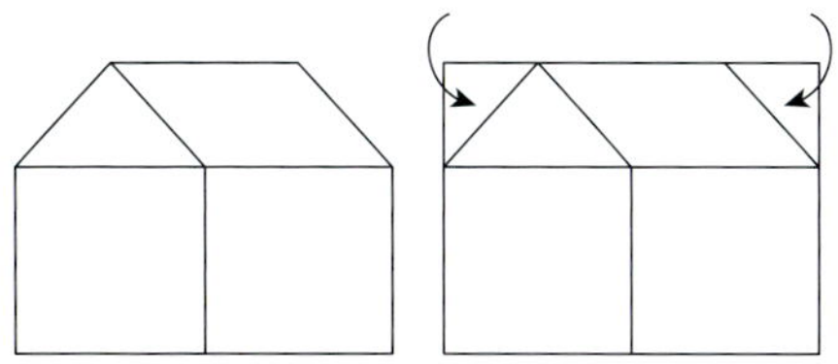

STEP 2

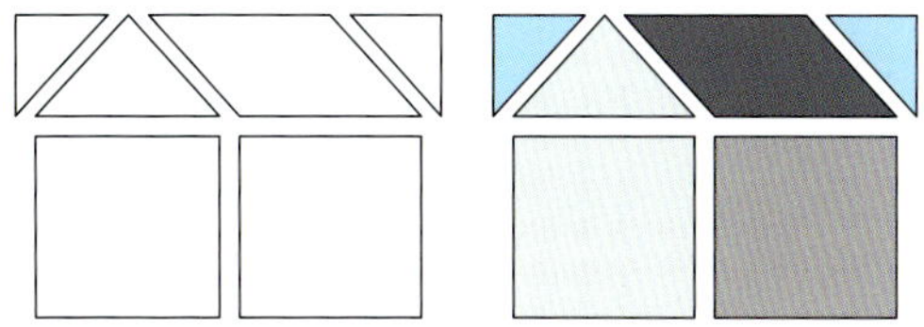

STEP 3

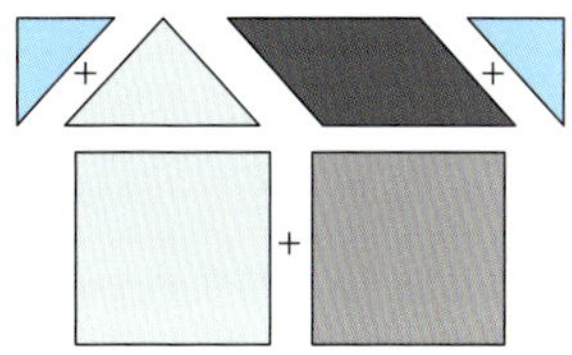

STEP 5

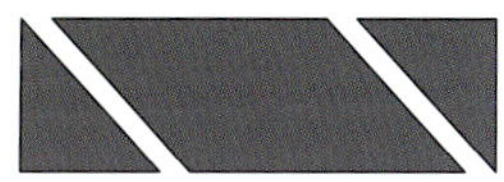

STEP 6

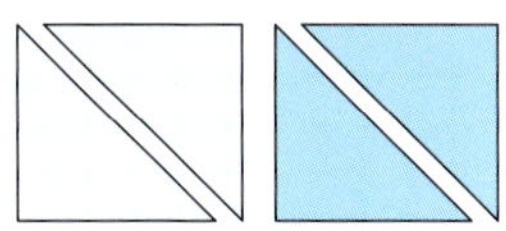

STEP 7

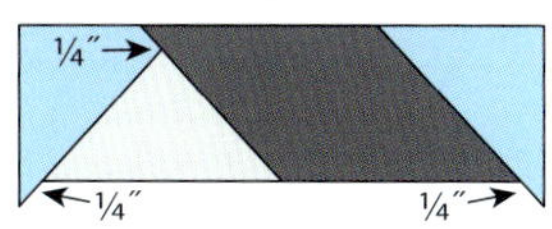

STEP 8

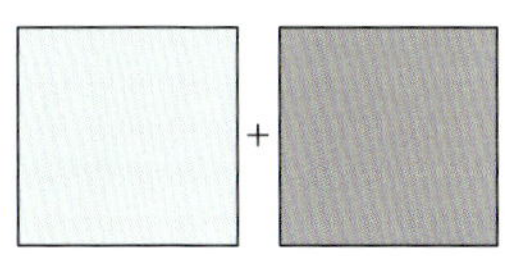

STEP 9

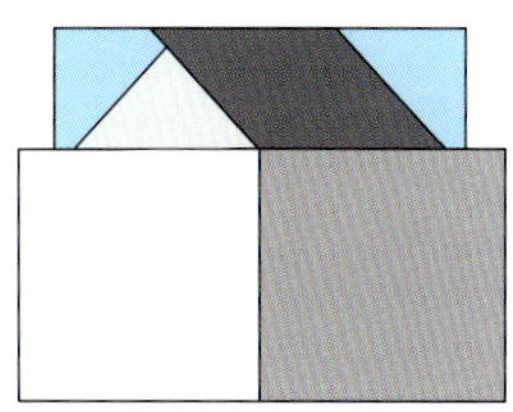

10 Align the tape on your Reveal Ruler with the roof points, and trim each side to leave a ¼″ seam allowance.

11 Add a bridge between the bottom of the house and the ground. Before adding the bridge, decide how tall you'd like your house to be and, using your Reveal Ruler, trim it to size. Add a bridge to the bottom of the house (see Bridges, page 28) and then add the ground piece.

12 Sew a background section using the same sky, bridge, and ground fabric to finish the same height and width as the house block. Place the bridge approximately halfway up from the bottom edge.

13 Slice the piece in half vertically and sew 1 piece to the right and left sides of the house. Add a top sky piece last, press your house, and trim to whatever size you'd like.

STEP 10

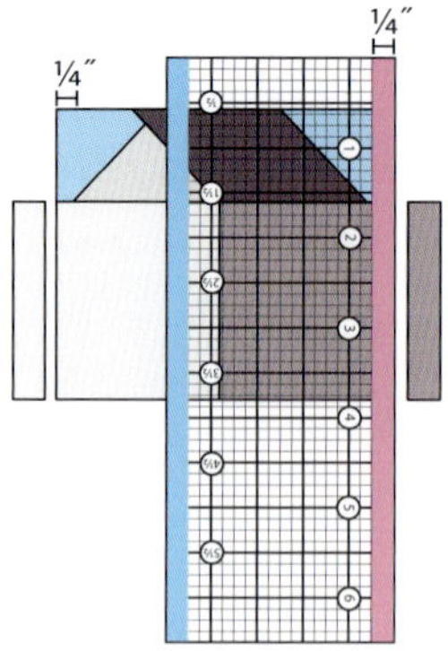

Trim edges ¼″ from roof points on each side.

STEP 11

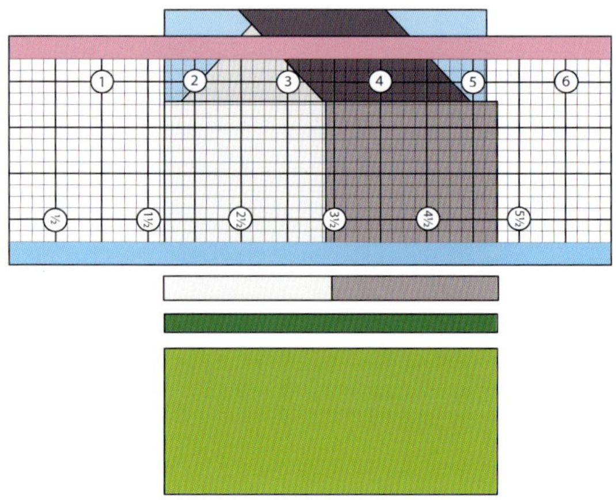

STEP 12

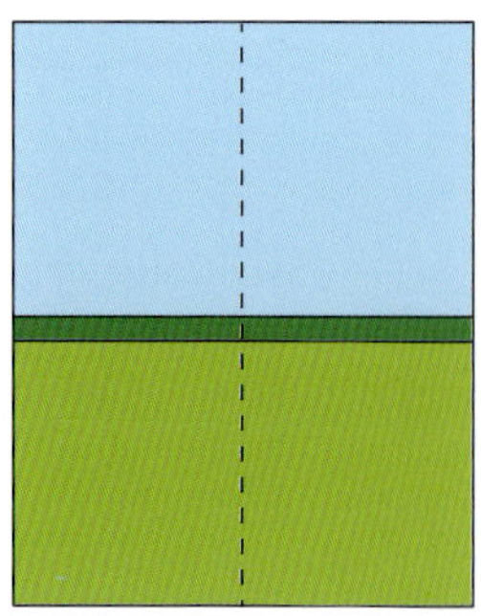

STEP 13

Simple Neighborhood, 37 × 15½″, by Karla Alexander, 2024

Advanced Houses and Neighborhoods

When you're making more intricate houses with windows and doors and assembling neighborhoods, the piecing isn't much different from making a simple house or a Log Cabin block. Start with a sketch, carefully plan your piecing order, and use your Reveal Ruler. With smaller pieces comes more intricacy, so make sure your fabrics have high contrast because it's easy for tiny pieces to disappear. It's worth your time to choose wisely.

Rustic Haven, 4″ × 5″, by Karla Alexander, 2024

A variety of windows and doors

Complex Houses

1 As you did for a simple house, draw a sketch of your house, separate the pieces, select your fabrics, and then determine your piecing order. Always overestimate the size of your pieces as they can be trimmed down as you go.

STEP 1

Townhouse Towers, 5½″ × 4¾″, by Karla Alexander, 2024

2 Piece together the window section.

3 Add the top house section to the window and use your Reveal Ruler to trim the windows to size.

4 Add the bottom house section and use your Reveal Ruler to trim the right and left sides of the house.

5 Add the side sections to the center window section and trim to size.

6 Add the side background piece on the left side of the house and then cut the roof at your desired angle.

7 Add the roof and trim to your desired size.

8 Assemble the chimney section separately. Layer the house over the chimney section and mark the roof angle. Align your Reveal Ruler so that the line you marked is just inside the reveal and trim.

9 Add the chimney section to the top of the house block.

10 Add the remaining background piece to the right side of the block.

11 Add the ground section to the bottom, press your house block, and trim to whatever size you'd like.

STEP 2

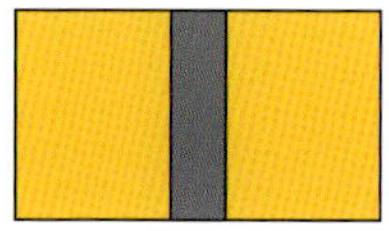

STEP 3

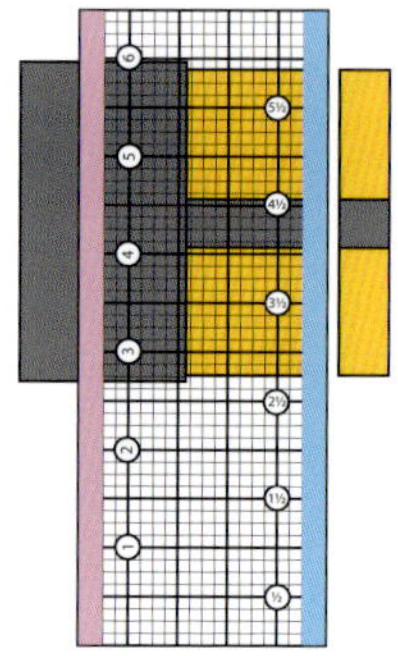

STEP 4

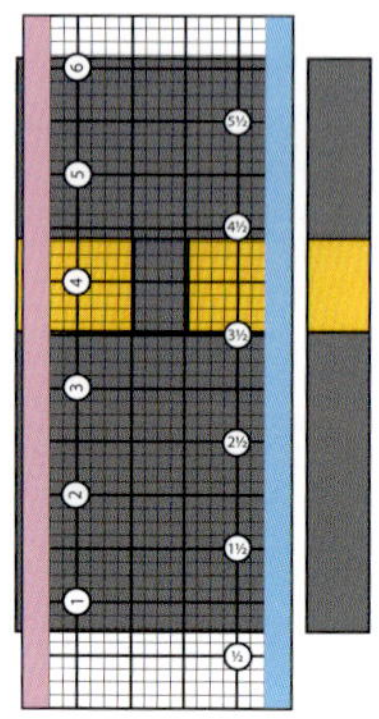

STEP 5

STEP 6

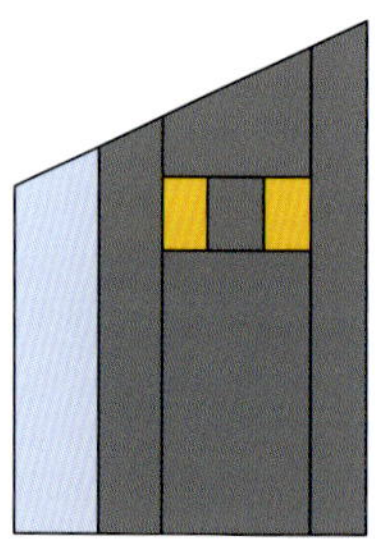

STEP 7

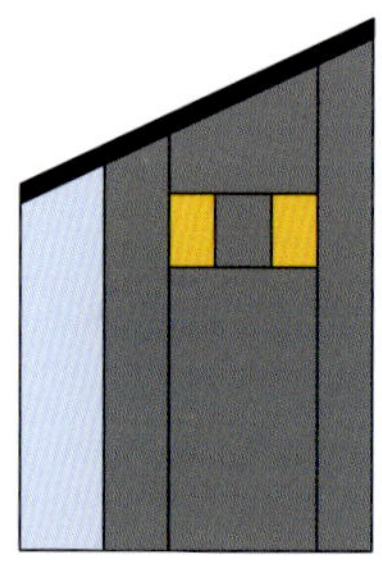

STEP 8

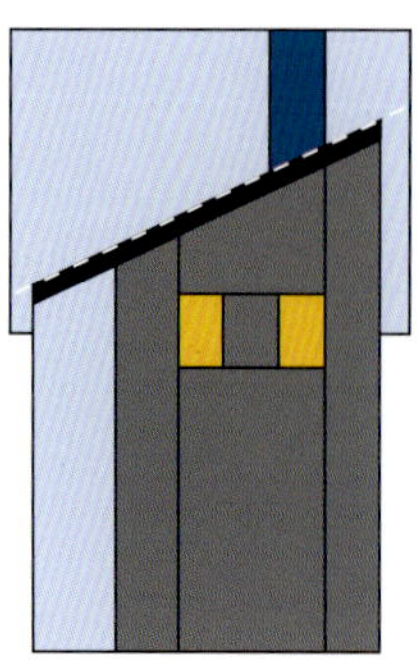

STEP 9

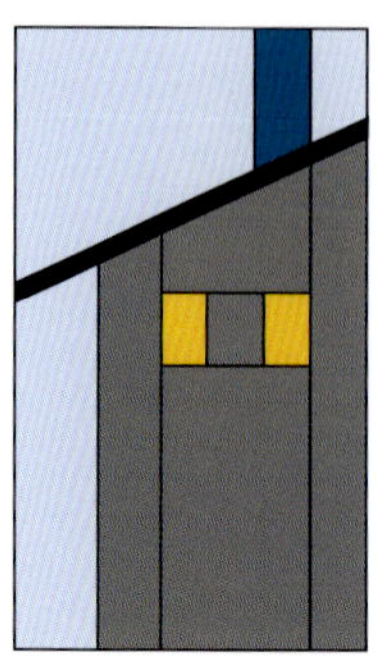

STEP 11

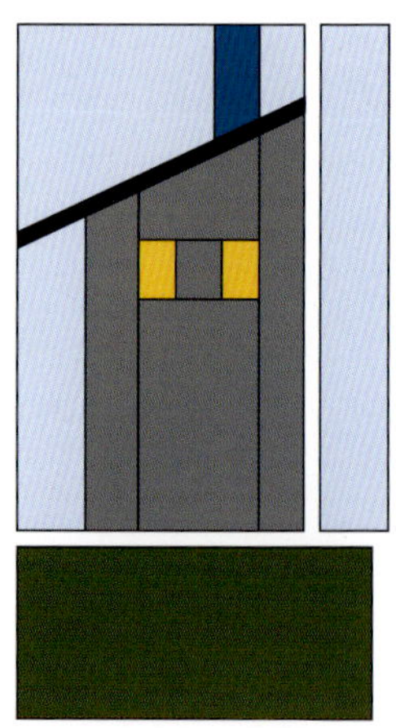

Neighborhoods

Now that you know how to make houses, you can construct neighborhoods. Make a collection of houses and audition several different arrangements. Decide whether you want them one next to the other or maybe some space in between. Play around a bit and have fun!

Once you have your arrangement, it will be clear where you need sky and ground, and you can fill in with the necessary pieces. You can also include additional elements (page 44).

The Village, 9¾″ × 6½″, by Karla Alexander, 2021

STACKED HOUSE NEIGHBORHOODS

Why stick to the mundane? If you can imagine it and sketch it, you can make it in miniature. Try stacking houses to give the appearance of townhomes or a city.

The Manor Resort, 8″ × 7¾″, by Karla Alexander, 2024

Blue Sky Condos, 7″ × 6″, by Karla Alexander, 2024

ADDITIONAL ELEMENTS

Country Cabin, 5¾″ × 4″, by Karla Alexander, 2024
A slightly complex house with trees

Mountains

Little mountains can be made in any size. Their size will change depending on the size of the fabric pieces you select. Choose several dark small-scale prints for the base of the mountain, along with one or more contrasting colors to represent snow. For the background, choose small-scale prints with values that contrast with the base and snow fabrics. Keep your choices close by and trim to size as you sew.

1 Choose approximately 5 mountain base colors in dark blues and purples, 3 light colors for the snow, and 1 background color. Cut strips of base and snow fabrics approximately 3″ × 4½″.

2 Pair 1 base and 1 snow strip right sides up, layer, and trim off one end at an angle. Sew a base piece to a snow piece. Finger-press the seams toward the dark fabric. Make 3 or 4 base/snow strips.

3 Position the sets into a stack to create a mountain. Rearrange in several combinations, overlapping with the snow sections at the top. Trim extra pieces to fill in as needed.

4 Lift the left section from the stack and place the Reveal Ruler on top. Rotate the ruler at an angle until you are satisfied with the result and trim along the right edge.

5 Move on to the next piece, align its left edge with the trimmed edge of the first piece and sew together. Trim the right edge as desired. Make sure to use the Reveal Ruler so the ¼″ seam allowance is automatically added.

6 Continue trimming and adjusting the pieces in this manner until the mountain is complete. If needed, trim the left and right edges, creating a point at the top, and press.

7 Center the mountain block on top of the background fabric, with the bottom edges aligned. Cut along the right and left edges of the mountain and then discard the center background triangle.

8 Align the bottom edges, sew the left background piece to the mountain, and finger-press the seam allowance toward the background. Align the bottom edges (the tip will overlap at the top) and sew the right background piece to the mountain. Press the seam allowance toward the mountain. Trim to desired block size and shape.

STEP 2

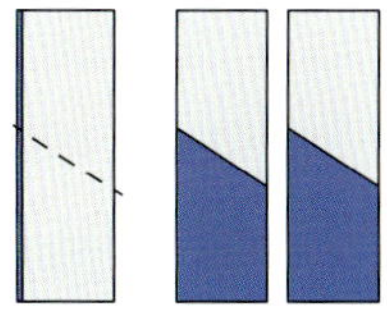

STEP 3

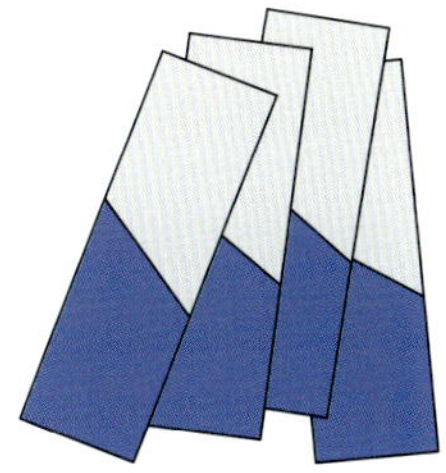

STEP 4

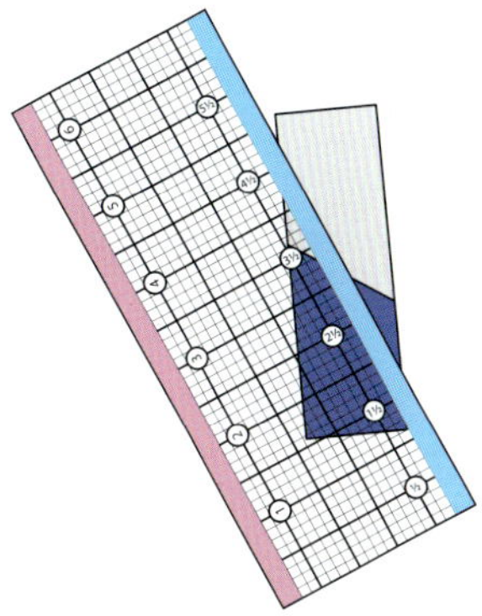

STEP 5

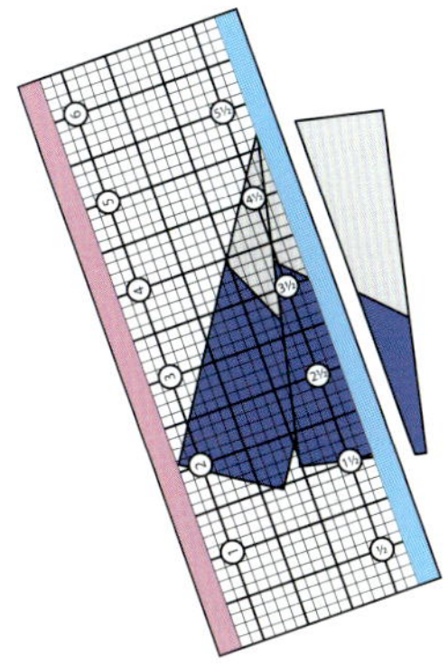

STEP 6

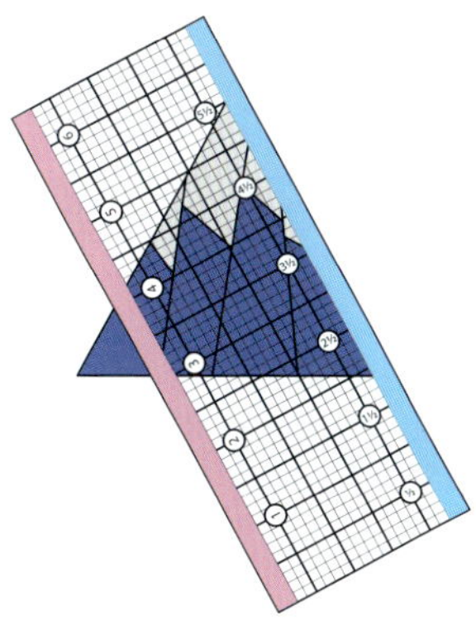

STEP 7

STEP 8

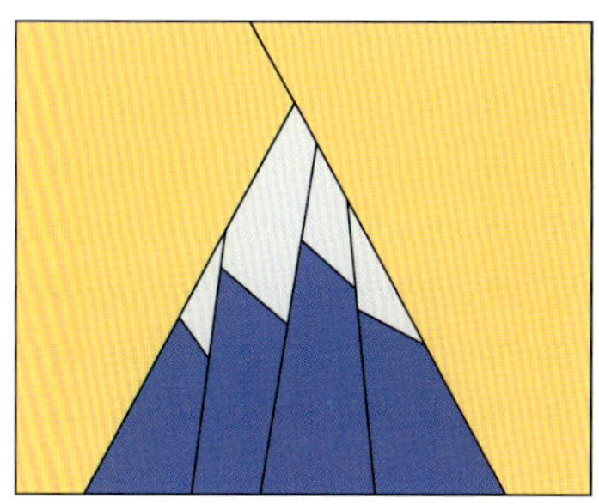

Trees

You can use the Reveal Method to make a variety of different trees. I like to make tiny triangle trees to finish at approximately 1½″ × 2½″ or smaller to use with my house blocks or on other small projects, such as greeting cards or quilt labels. I make larger trees with more piecework for larger projects, such as place mats and wall hangings.

Tree sizes are easy to modify by adjusting the size of the beginning pieces. Make a simple tree by using only one piece of fabric trimmed into the shape of a tree without added piecework or consider using festive prints, such as Christmas or Halloween themes, for a wall hanging or greeting card. Use your imagination and try different solid and pieced backgrounds for a light, bright sky or a dark, quiet, midnight feel. Trees are a lot of fun to make and, depending on how many pieces you use, sew together quickly.

TIP

A fat eighth of your selected colors will be adequate yardage for trees. I suggest gathering a group of the colors you need for all the positions—branches, trunk, sky, and ground—and keeping them next to you as you sew, trimming pieces to size as needed.

Triangle Tree

1 Gather 4 strips of green fabric approximately 1½″ × 3″. Arrange the strips in a pleasing order with good contrast. Sew the first 2 pieces together and finger-press the seam toward the first piece.

2 Leave the first piece untrimmed. Use your Reveal Ruler to trim the second piece to approximately ⅛″. Remember, the ruler will automatically add the seam allowance.

3 Add Pieces 3 and 4 in the same manner, each time trimming to a different width and pressing toward the previous piece. Do not trim the fourth piece; you will adjust it once the side pieces are added.

STEP 1

STEP 2

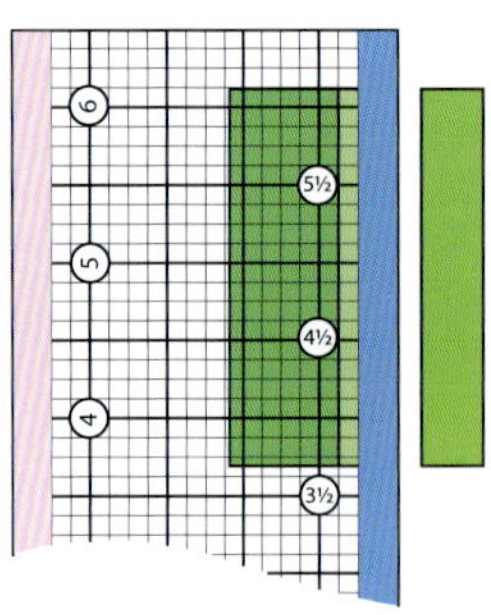

STEP 3

4 Arrange the patchwork with the seams positioned horizontally. Place your ruler on top at an angle to create the right half of the tree and trim the excess. The wider the angle, the wider the finished tree will be.

5 Lay the trimmed tree on top of the background piece, leaving ¼″ between the top of the tree and the top of the background. Place the ruler on top of the tree and trim the background, copying the angle of the tree.

6 Sew the trimmed background piece to the right side of the tree. Don't worry if it doesn't match the length of the tree; it will be trimmed in the steps below.

7 Repeat Steps 5 and 6 to add another background piece. When trimming the left side, use the Reveal Ruler and slide it up and down to audition the shape of the tree and determine how much of the first top green piece you want to show. Swing the ruler out at the bottom for a wider tree. Be sure to leave ¼″ above the tip of the tree for the seam allowance. Sew the background piece to the left side of the tree.

8 Trim the bottom of the tree block straight to the desired height. Press and set aside.

9 For the trunk, sew a brown trunk piece to a background piece and trim with the Reveal Ruler to approximately ¼″ or your desired width. Finger-press toward the background and then add the right background piece. Finger-press the seam toward the trunk.

10 Center the trunk section along the bottom of the tree block and sew in place. *Optional:* Add a green piece to the bottom for ground or any other piecework desired.

STEP 4

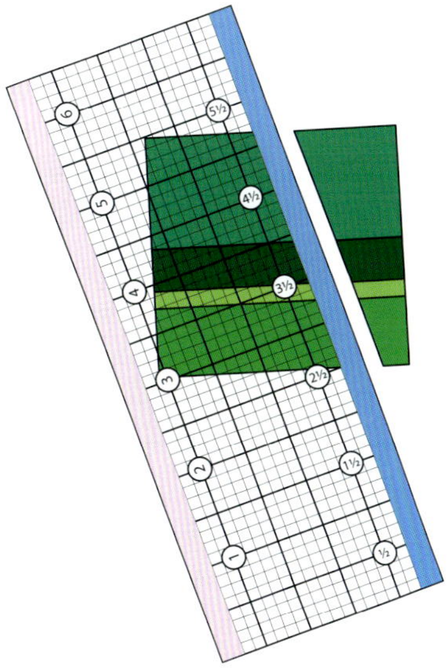

STEP 5

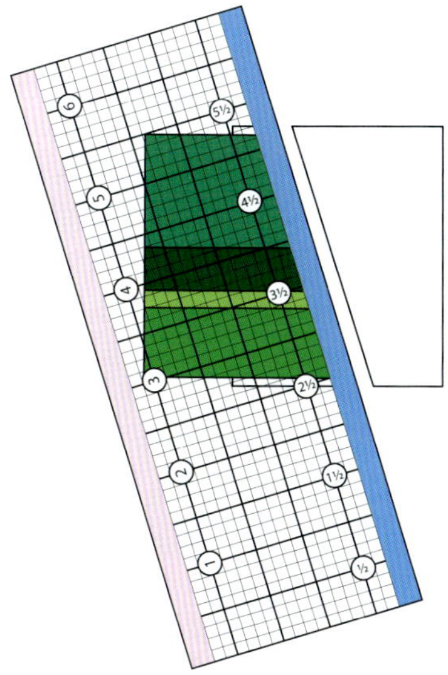

STEP 7

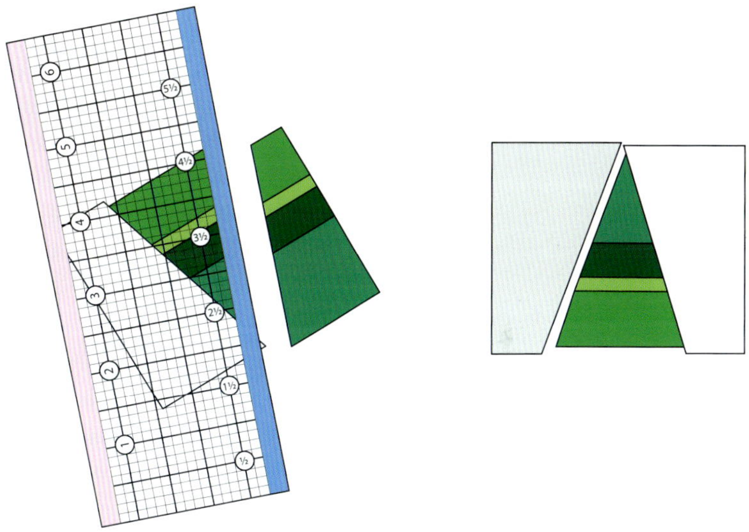

STEP 8

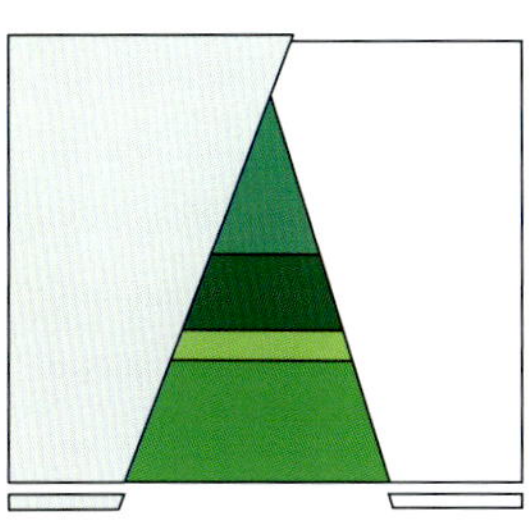

STEP 9

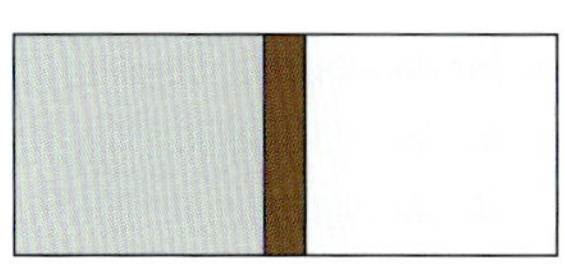

STEP 10

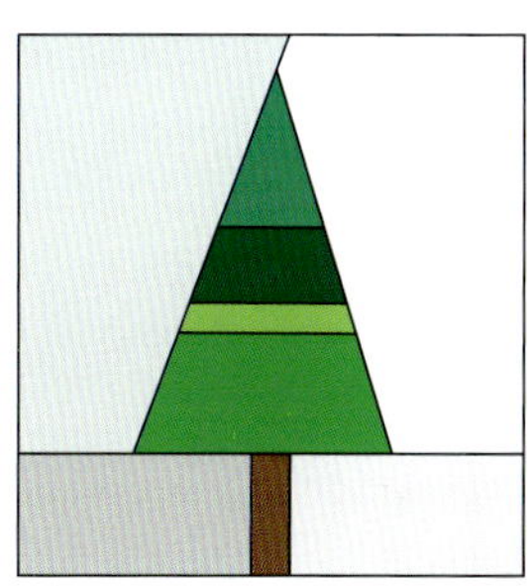

Triangle Tree Variation

This variation has some piecework that can be adjusted as desired. Different prints, such as small-scale polka dots or stripes, make a fun addition, or try making a black and white or red tree for a whimsical look. Use your imagination when it comes to colors and piecework. Add a star button at the top for a Christmas tree or piece it in orange and black for some Halloween flair.

Rather than making your tree from the top down, work from the center out. Make sure your center strip is a minimum of ¼″ at the top and wider at the bottom. Alternate adding strips on the left and right. When you add the left piece, it should always overlap the top of the right piece. Press the seams away from the center piece. Use your Reveal Ruler to trim each piece after it is added, angling the piece so it is wider at the bottom and narrower at the top, leaving a minimum of ¼″ width at the top for the seam allowance. Make each angle different as you go, evening them out as you add strips. Continue until your tree is the desired size.

Trim the block straight across the bottom and construct and add a trunk section. Add background sections to either side of the tree.

Stacked Triangle Tree

1 Stack 3 green tree rectangles right side up, with the short edges to the right and left. The fabric order doesn't matter.

2 Place the Reveal Ruler on the stack at an angle, with the right edge centered at the top and the bottom slid to the corner, creating the angle of your tree. Trim along the edge of the ruler and discard the corner pieces.

STEP 1

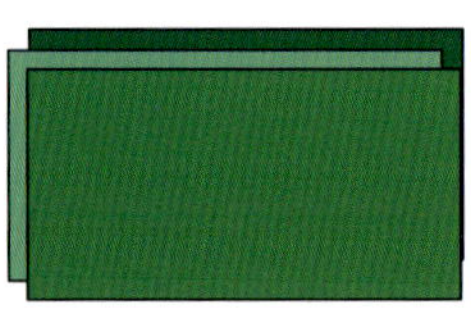

STEP 2

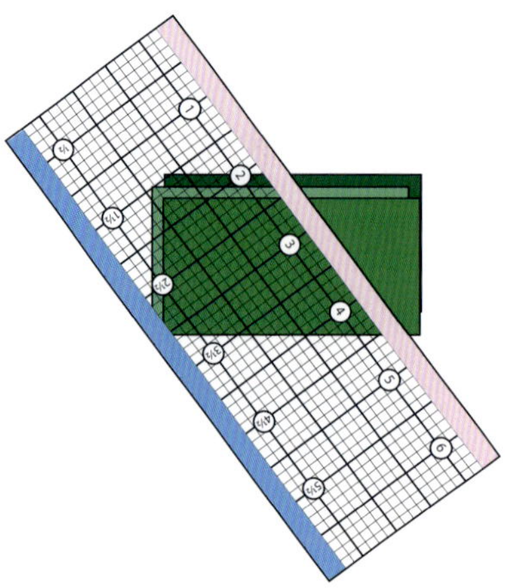

3 Repeat Step 2, but this time, rotate the stack 180°. Match the ruler with the center cut, swing the end of the ruler to the right until you are satisfied with the angle, and then trim along the edge.

4 Stack the background rectangles right side up, with the short edges to the right and left. Center one of the trimmed tree pieces on top, aligning the bottom edge with the bottom edge of the stack. Align the ruler with the right edge of the green piece and cut along this edge first. Shift those pieces out of the way, then cut along the left edge, creating the background sections.

5 Pair, align, and sew a left background piece to the left side of a green tree section. Finger-press the seam toward the tree piece. Repeat with a right background piece on the right side, making sure to overlap at the top to keep a minimum ¼″ seam allowance above the point of the tree. Finger-press toward the background. Repeat to make the 2 remaining tree sections.

6 For a straight tree, stack the 3 tree sections. Trim the bottom edge of all 3 sections even with the green edges. Place your ruler across the tops of the middle and bottom sections and trim. For these sections, it is okay to cut off the point. Sew all 3 sections together and press the seams to one side.

For a crooked tree, angle the center section and overlap the top and bottom sections. Adjust them to audition the final look. Trim the angles on the center tree section. Place the top section beneath the center section and use your ruler to match and trim the angle. Repeat for the bottom section. Sew all 3 sections together and press the seams to one side.

7 For the trunk, sew a brown trunk piece to a background piece and trim with the Reveal Ruler to approximately ¼″ or your desired width. Finger-press toward the background and then add the right background piece. Finger-press the seam toward the trunk.

8 Center the trunk section along the bottom of the tree block and sew in place. Trim the tree block into a rectangle, making sure to leave ¼″ of background around each tree tip for the seam allowance.

STEP 3

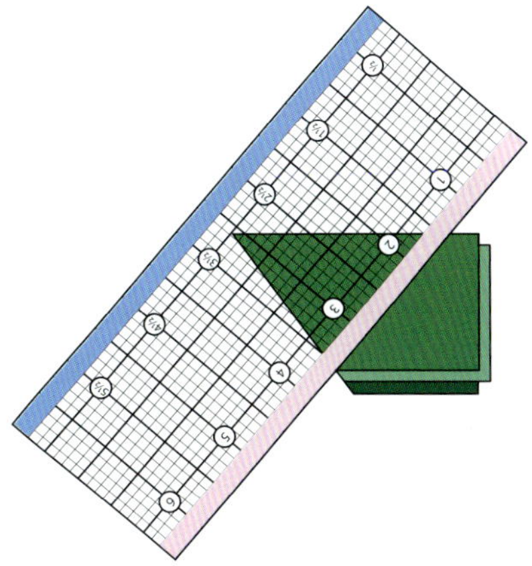

STEP 4

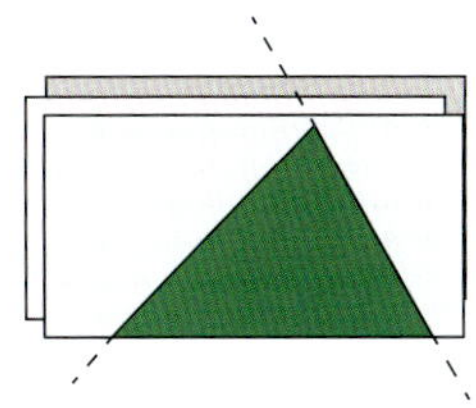

STEP 5

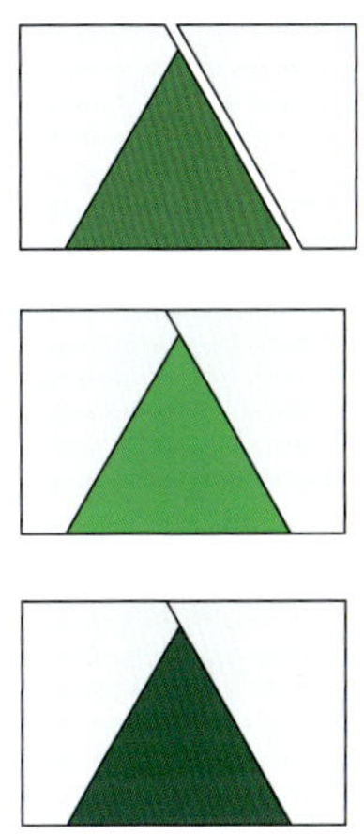

STEP 6

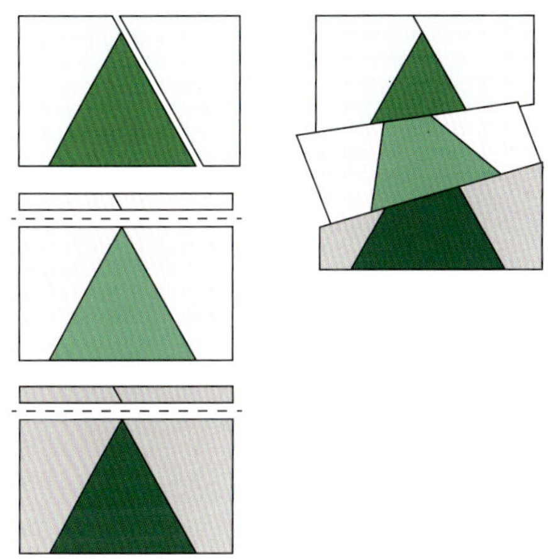

STEP 7

STEP 8

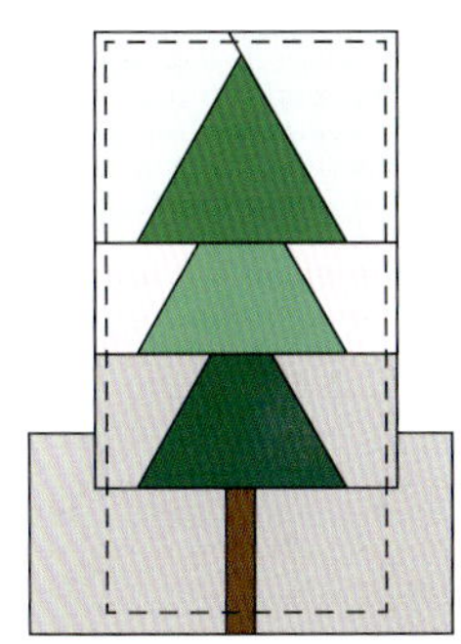

Round Improv Tree

This tree and its variation are similarly shaped, just with different piecework. You can significantly enhance the look by adding complex details with tiny bridges of deep red, purple, or chartreuse or by choosing to use either a solid or pieced background.

1 Gather a variety of green scraps approximately 2″ × 4″ in a range of values from light to dark, a variety of white, gray, and tan small-scale print scraps approximately 5″ × 6″, and a brown scrap 1½″ × 4″.

2 Layer the green rectangles in a stack and cut in half diagonally. Layer the white, gray, and tan scraps into a stack and cut in half diagonally.

3 Choose 2 contrasting green pieces for the center of the tree, sew right sides together, and then finger-press the seam to one side. Place the Reveal Ruler on top, positioned with the taped edge crossing over the seam allowance. Rotate the ruler right or left until you find a small section you like **under the ruler** that will begin the improv-like patchwork. Once you are satisfied with the result, trim along the taped edge of the ruler.

4 Choose another green piece, sew it to the last cut edge, and finger-press the seams to one side. Place the ruler on top, rotating it right, left, up, or down until you are satisfied with the result, and then trim along the taped edge.

STEP 2

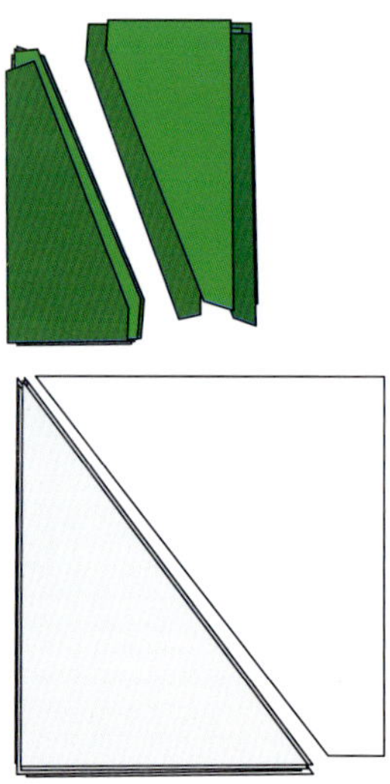

STEP 3

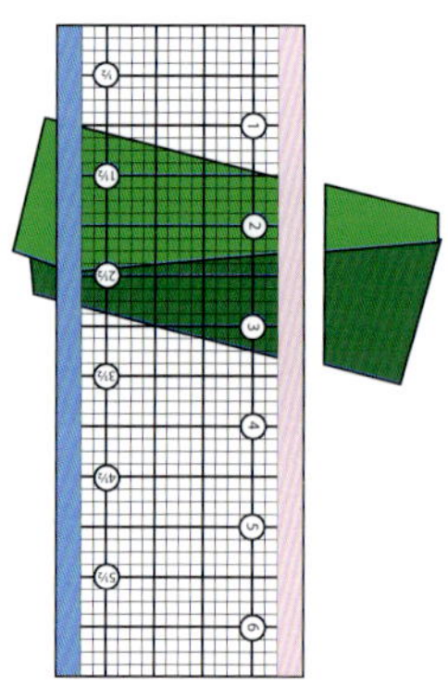

STEP 4

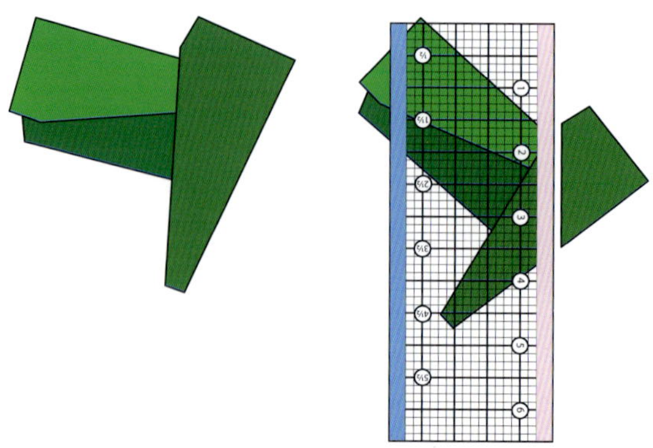

5 Continue adding pieces in a circular motion, placing the ruler on top each time so you can plan the result, and then trim. Trim each piece differently for an organic result. Add as many pieces as you'd like until you are happy with the size and shape, including ¼″ seam allowance around the outer edge. For small projects, I like the tree body to finish at approximately 2½″ tall, and I decide on the width as I go, adding extra pieces as necessary.

6 Add the background to the right, left, and top of the tree in the same manner as the green pieces to create a framework around the tree to reach the desired size.

7 Once the piecing is complete, trim the tree straight on all sides and set aside.

8 To piece the bottom half of the tree, sew a 1″ × 1½″ background strip to a 1″ green strip. Finger-press the seams toward the green fabric. Make 2 sets.

9 Place the Reveal Ruler across the seam of 1 set and trim the edge at a slight angle.

10 Cut a 1″ × 2″ strip of brown fabric for a short branch and sew to the trimmed edge. Use the ruler to trim the branch to approximately ¼″ width.

STEP 5

STEP 7

STEP 9

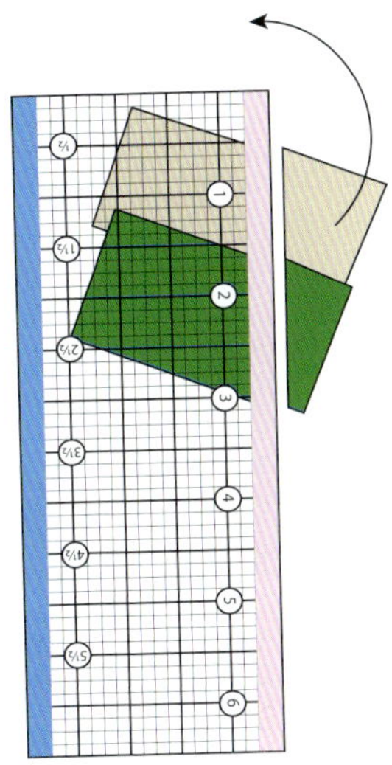

STEP 10

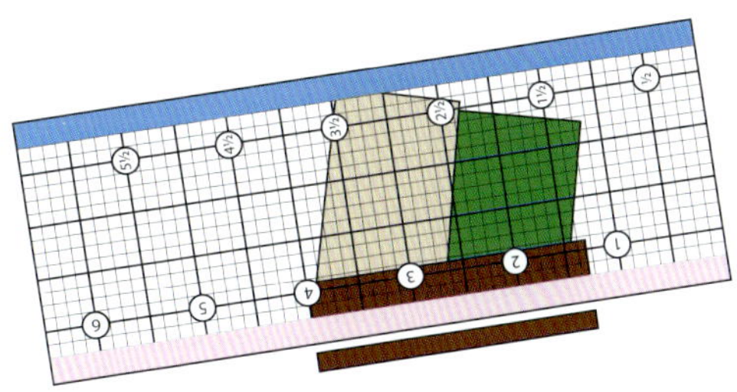

11 Add the second tree/background set to the trimmed edge. Pretrim the angle of the new set, if necessary, to roughly align with the first set on the other side of the branch piece. Finger-press the seam toward the branch. Place the Reveal Ruler on top of the combination at an angle, adjusting the reveal to prepare the edge for the second, longer branch.

12 Cut a second brown strip to 1″ × 2″ and sew to the trimmed edge, connecting with the first branch. Trim the width of the branch to approximately ¼″ and then add a light background triangle. Continue adding background pieces to build on the left side. Set the left section aside.

13 To build the right side, start with a 1½″ × 2″ green rectangle.

14 Continue building the right side by adding background triangles. Add enough pieces to create a rectangle matching the length of the left section. Align the right and left sections side by side and check to see that the green pieces roughly line up. Add extra greenery to the top, if needed.

15 Trim the inner edges of both sections at a slightly outward angle so the trunk will finish a tiny bit wider at the bottom and narrower at the top. Cut a brown trunk piece into a strip 1″ wide. The length should match the background pieces.

16 Sew the trunk piece to the left half and press the seams toward the trunk. Use the Reveal Ruler to determine the right side angle of the trunk and trim. Use the ruler agin to double check that the right edge of the trunk matches the angle of the right background section. Sew the 2 pieces together, and press the seams toward the trunk. Trim the bottom section straight across the top.

17 Center the combined bottom half beneath the top tree section, pin, and sew together. Press the seams to one side. Trim to desired block size and shape.

STEP 11

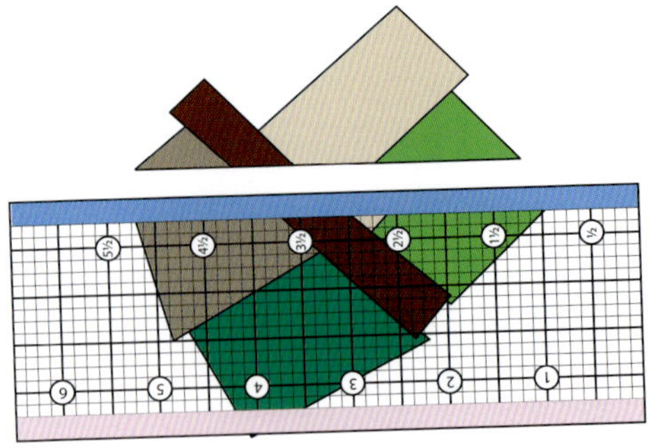

STEP 12

STEP 14

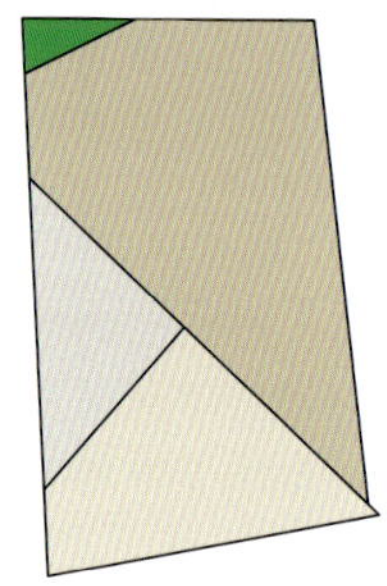

STEP 16

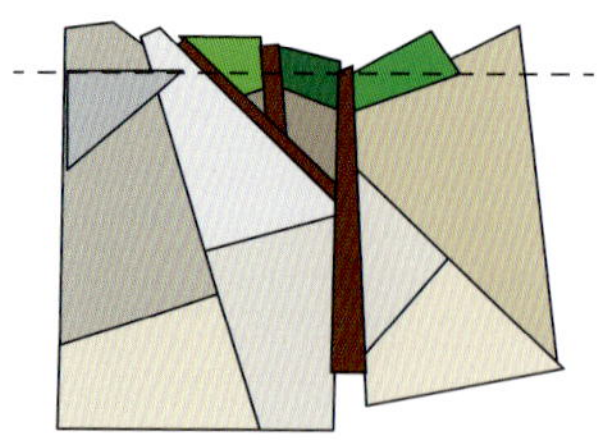

STEP 17

Round Strip Tree Variation

This alternative take requires making a simple patchwork of unequal vertical strips instead of working in a circular fashion. For variety, try adding additional narrow pieces or interesting bridges, making a smaller tree block and sewing it to the top of the first to create a taller tree, or choosing a solid color or pieced background.

Using your Reveal Ruler, randomly cut and piece a variety of fabric strips. Stitch them together side by side and a few end to end, combining them until you have a rectangle of the desired size. Trim off all 4 corners of the block, varying angles as desired. Use your Reveal Ruler to see and review the result before trimming. Sew a background triangle to each corner.

Follow Steps 8–17 to add a trunk to your tree body.

Stick (Leafless) Trees

I call these leafless trees "stick trees," and once you learn the basic concept, you can move on to make more complex trees. For all trees, the sky and ground backgrounds are the same, and the branch piecework is done by using your Reveal Ruler.

When choosing fabric for the trees, look for small-scale prints with interesting patterns and textures. Add a small number of interesting dark colors to use as accents. Choose any color you'd like for the background, but make sure it's a good contrast from the tree branches.

1 For the trunk and branches, gather 4–6 light-value small-scale prints and 4–6 dark-value small-scale prints. Choose a medium-gray fabric for the background.

2 Cut the fabric for the trunk and branches into 2″ × 12″ strips. Cut the background into a 12″ × 12″ square.

3 Build the trunk and branches by cutting the 2″ strips into 2″–3″ lengths. Sew 6–7 pairs of dark and light strips together along their short ends. As you sew, finger-press the seams toward the dark fabric. Trim and build different combinations by adding sections together with a few accent bridges along the way. Trim branch pieces to 1½″ wide and trunk pieces to 2″ wide. The lengths can be increased or decreased as the background is added. Make 6 branch combinations.

4 Trim a 1½″ strip from one end of the background fabric and subcut into 2″ lengths. Sew a 2″ background piece to one end of each branch combination. Press the seams to one side.

5 Refer to the diagram and cut the background in half. Cut each half apart according to the diagram (or create your own). Separate and slide each piece out of the way as it is cut.

6 Build the tree by piecing the background together with branches, in the opposite order from which it was cut. Choose one pieced branch and sew it to the last cut background piece (1). Add extra length, if needed. Use your Reveal Ruler to show ½″ of the branch underneath the ruler and trim. As you sew, press the seams toward the branches. Add the next piece of background (2) and press.

7 Continue adding the branches and background in numerical order as shown. The seams should fold together and meet on the backside just as the original background piece was cut apart.

8 Once the right side is complete, set it aside and repeat piecing on the left side. Press both halves.

9 Trim the center trunk at a slight angle so the bottom width is 1¾″ and the top is 1½″. You can also choose a different angle.

10 Place the 2 halves side by side and trim a ¼″ angle from the lower-inside right and left edges to create a wider space for the bottom of the trunk. Pin and sew the trunk between the right and left halves and press the seams toward the trunk.

STEP 3

STEP 4

STEP 5

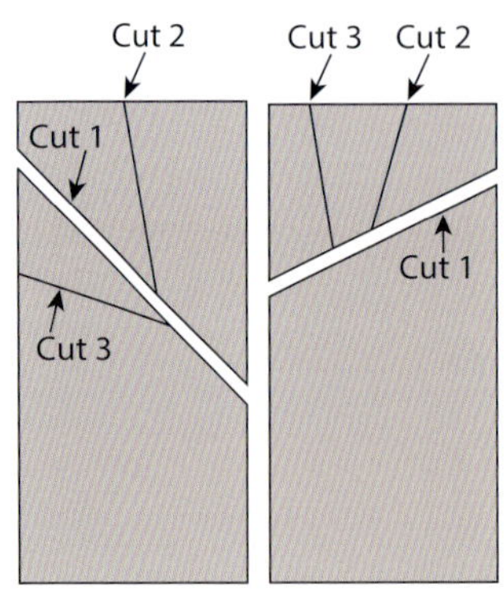

STEP 6

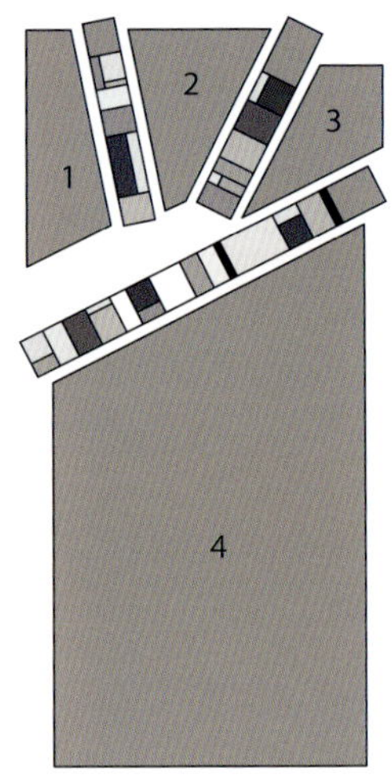

STEP 8

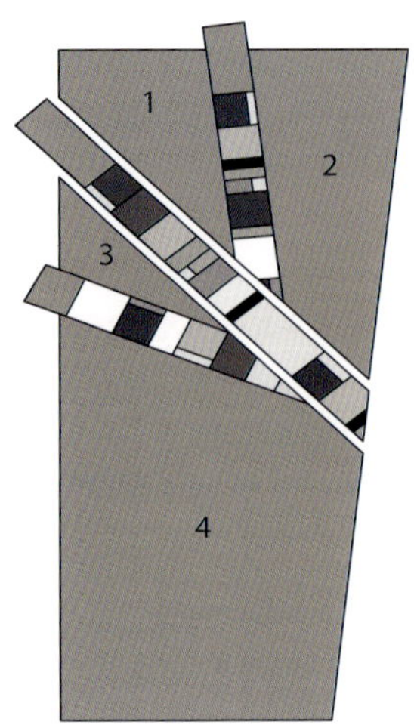

STEP 10

Stick (Leafless) Tree Variation

Now that you have the basic construction method, you can branch out, so to speak. For a more complex tree, you'll vary the widths of the trunk and branches, which in turn will change all the background measurements. It takes a bit more time and patience, but the results are well worth it. The height, number of branches, and piecework can match the book samples, or you can go out on a limb. Have fun, use your imagination, and build a forest!

Old Birch Tree, 14″ × 18″, by Karla Alexander, 2024

In this example, I did a little improv piecing of the ground to achieve curves.

Sky and Ground

When your block requires that the background represent sky or ground, audition your fabric to find an interesting piece that can do the job for you. You might find a blue print with swirls representing clouds or wind, or a green or brown fabric with little dots or lines to give the appearance of grass. These would all make good choices.

Ocean Estates, 17″ × 9″, by Karla Alexander, 2024

The gray background fabric looks just like a road or sandy beach.

Sometimes, a background has just what you need.

However, you can also build the sky or ground yourself! When you're piecing Littles, such as houses and trees, sometimes it's nice to add extra piecework in the sky or ground background sections, making the finished piece even more appealing.

Gather a variety of fabrics in the colorway you need, cut the pieces, and sew them back together in sections. Combine the sections, building them into a larger unit. Trim sections as you go so they fit well together. Periodically stop to make sure you are happy with the results, adding pieces and bridges until the piece is the desired size.

The finished sections can be as simple or complex as you like. Consider your intended use to make the piecing decisions. Add bridges (page 28) where you feel they will add interest. For a bridge, I often enjoy using a small-scale black and white strip with stripes or polka dots.

Aerial View, 10″ × 11″, by Karla Alexander, 2025

APPLICATIONS

Unfiltered, 56″ × 74″, by Karla Alexander, 2024

Now that you know how to make a wide variety of Littles, it's time to consider ways to add them to your projects. You can also finish them as stand-alone blocks and show them off any way you want.

Four single blocks finished as trivets

Momentum Octo, 6½″ × 6½″, by Karla Alexander, 2024

Spokes, 6¼″ × 6″, by Karla Alexander, 2024

Bridge, 7″ × 6″, by Karla Alexander, 2025

Between the Lines, 7″ × 7½″, by Karla Alexander, 2025

Business card holder

To decorate a pocket tissue cover

On a carry bag for your rotary cutter

To make a gift bag as appreciated as the contents

Full Moon, 8¼″ × 10″, by Karla Alexander, 2025
Mounted as a wall hanging

Adding Littles to Your Quilt Top

Littles make a great addition to quilts of any size. Audition your projects as you go and decide where you can add or where you might need more action. Choose these spaces for additional piecework.

A fun way to spruce up your quilts is to work a variety of little blocks and bridges into the border. This works with traditional quilts and, of course, fits in with improvisational quilts. For a traditional quilt, I suggest choosing a border corner to build in an area of Littles.

Dave, 21″ × 25″, by Karla Alexander, 2023

I also like to add Littles as cornerstones in the sashing of my quilts. To do this, first check out the blocks that are in your quilt. For example, if the quilt is made up of half-square triangles, it would work well to make miniature blocks that are similar and don't take away too much focus from the main blocks. Check the required sashing width so you know what size to make the blocks. Next, decide whether you want to copy the colors in the main blocks or add a new splash of color.

Often, the scale of the fabric in the original blocks is too big for Littles, so you may need to search through your leftovers or stash to find fabric that works better. Once you have the target size and fabric selected, decide how many blocks to make.

Once your blocks are done, you need to integrate them into your quilt top. Imagine your quilt top as a grid: You want to replace a grid section, part of a section, or more with your Littles. Use through lines (page 19) to deconstruct the design and see where you can add your blocks. You may need to adjust the size by trimming or adding some background. Just be sure to use your Reveal Ruler when trimming so you don't lose your seam allowance.

Mountain View Village, 11½″ × 22½″, by Karla Alexander, 2023

Crafting Letters

Using the Reveal method to piece letters works well and provides another useful technique.

Anything from a child's name to a quote can be built into a wall hanging or added to a quilt top. To begin, figure out which letters and how many of each letter are needed as well as the target size of the text you want to add.

Choose the fabrics for the letters along with a contrasting background. For the background, I usually use a mix of scraps or fat quarters in light prints and then cut them into 3″ strips to use as I go.

Sketch the letters on paper and draw lines where sections intersect. Just as you would with any block, use through lines to deconstruct the letter to determine the piecing order. Most letters consist of straight angled lines, but for the letters C, G, O, Q, and S you will need some additional piecing. For letters that require curves, add straight angled lines to approximate the curve. Follow the same process as with the straight-line letters, but with more pieces per letter.

When you have your fabric selected and your piecing order determined, roughly estimate the size of your first piece and use the Reveal Method to construct the letter. To practice this technique, jump ahead to the *Love Letters* wall hanging (page 75).

Mark Twain Focus, 50″ × 58″, by Karla Alexander, 2023

Projects

In this section, you'll find a variety of simple projects that will allow you to practice making Littles and incorporating them into your projects.

Using the Reveal Method, you won't need a lot of fabric for the Littles in each project. In the materials lists, I outline the fabric colors and approximate fabric sizes you'll need so you can gather the right fabrics and have them handy when you construct your block. Precutting pieces for Littles is unnecessary because the pieces are trimmed to size as you sew.

ECHO PINCUSHION

Finished pincushion: 7½″ × 7½″ × 1½″

This pincushion is not only useful and fun to make; it is the perfect gift for a quilter friend, especially when stuffed with lavender or filling sprinkled with essential oils. Weighted with aquarium sand to prevent it from being knocked to the floor, it also has a hard bottom, so no need to worry about being poked when picking it up. I keep this size pincushion on my ironing board, bristling with an array of different pins, and carry a smaller version with me as I travel from sewing machine, to cutting board, to retreats, and more!

Travel sized pincushion

Materials

Yardages are based on 40″-wide fabric.

If you choose to use your existing scraps or yardage, you can skip right to the cutting list to find the dimensions of the pieces you'll need.

For the center block, a stack of light and dark squares and strips will do the trick. Just prepare your selections, set them to the side so they are handy, and cut off sections as you go. You can re-create the sample pincushion by using the following list or choose a mix of contrasting solids or prints as desired.

Cranberry red for center square and Round 6: 4″ × 10″ rectangle

Medium green for Round 1: 4″ × 4″ square

Black for Round 2 and Round 7: 7″ × 10″ rectangle

Turquoise for Round 4: 4″ × 10″ rectangle

Bright yellow for Round 5: 4″ × 12″ rectangle

Medium gray for outer border: 10″ × 12″

Dark gray for Round 3 and base: ½ yard or 1 fat quarter

Fiberfill

Aquarium sand for weight: ½–¾ cup

Optional: Lightweight fusible polyester batting, 9″ × 9″

Optional: Lightweight cardboard for base, 6″ × 6″

Optional: Coordinating fabric scrap to cover cardboard, 7″ × 7″

Optional: Fabric glue for base

Cutting

Cranberry red: Cut 1 square 1″ × 1″. Set aside the remainder for Round 6.

Black: Cut 4 rectangles 1¼″ × 8″ for Round 7. Set aside the remainder for Round 2.

Medium gray: Cut 4 rectangles 2¼″ × 10″.

Dark gray: Cut 1 rectangle 9″ × 10″.

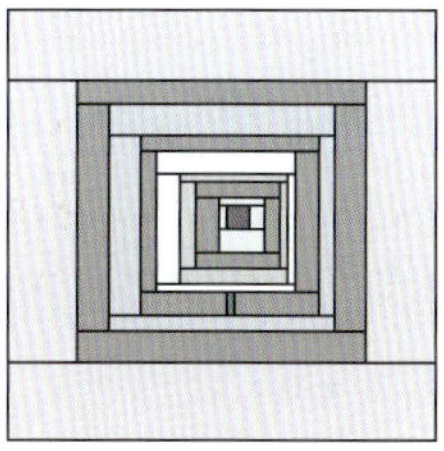

Center Block

1 Trim the medium green fabric into 2 squares approximately 1″ × 1″ and 2 rectangles approximately 1½″ × 2″. Sew the green squares to opposite sides of the cranberry square. Finger-press the seams toward the green and trim off the excess edges so they are even with the center square.

2 Add the 2 remaining green rectangles to the top and bottom edges. Finger-press the seams toward the green and trim off the excess edges. This step completes Round 1.

3 Place the piece you just made right side up and use your Reveal Ruler to show approximately ¼″ of the first green piece. Trim along the outer edge of the ruler. Roughly cut a piece of black to match the edge just trimmed and sew the black piece to the green. Finger-press the seam toward the black.

4 Place the unit right side up, with the new black piece on the left. Use your Reveal Ruler to show approximately ⅛″ of the green piece. Trim along the outer edge of the ruler. Roughly cut a piece of black to match the edge just trimmed and sew the black piece to the green. Finger-press the seam toward the black.

5 Place the piece you just made right side up, rotated so the black pieces are on the top and bottom. Use your Reveal Ruler to show approximately ⅛″ of the green piece on the right. Trim along the outer edge of the ruler. Roughly cut a piece of black to match the edge just trimmed and sew the black piece to the green. Finger-press the seam toward the black.

STEP 1

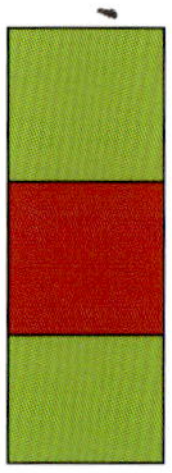

STEP 2

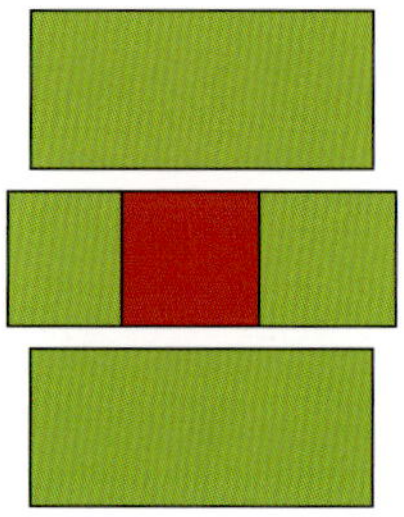

STEP 3

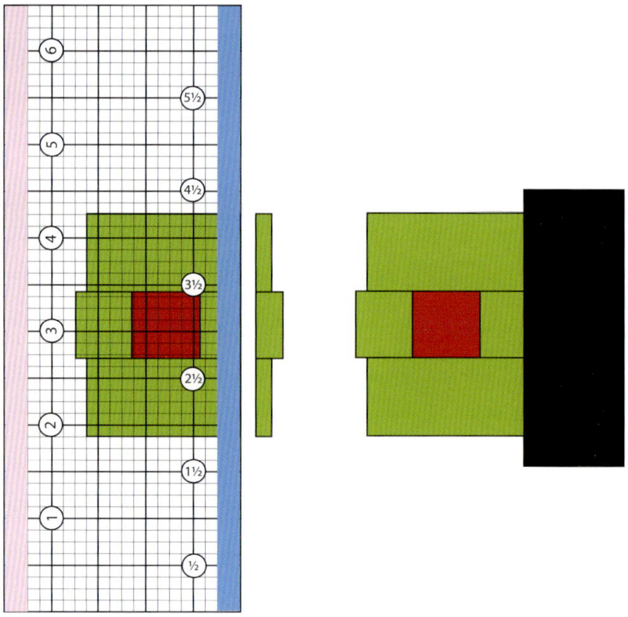

STEP 4

STEP 5

6 Place the piece you just made right side up and rotate so the black piece just added is on the left. Use your Reveal Ruler to show approximately ⅜″ of the green piece. Trim along the outer edge of the ruler. Roughly cut a piece of black to match the edge just trimmed and sew the black piece to the green. Finger-press the seam toward the black. This step completes Round 2.

7 Repeat Steps 3–6 by using the following colors and adding pieces in the following order. Trim each side of the previous round by using your Reveal Ruler to show that amount of fabric; remember that the ¼″ seam allowance will be automatically added when you trim along the edge of the ruler. Press the seams toward the newly added pieces as you go.

Round 3: Trim right ¼″, left ⅜″, top ¼″, bottom ¼″; add dark gray strips.

Round 4: Trim right ⅛″, left ⅜″, top ⅛″, bottom ⅜″; add turquoise strips.

Round 5: Trim right ⅛″, left ⅝″, top ⅝″, bottom ⅛″; add bright yellow strips.

Optional: Before adding the last yellow strip, I sewed a cranberry red bridge into the length of the yellow strip, and instead of using the same yellow on the other side, I swapped in a greenish-gold piece for a bit more interest.

Round 6: Trim right ⅝″, left ¼″, top ¼″, bottom ⅝″; add cranberry red strips.

Round 7: Trim right ¼″, left ¾″, top ¾″, bottom ¼″; add 1¼″ black strips.

Round 8: Add 2¼″ medium gray strips to the right and left sides and then trim the ends even with the patchwork. Add 2¼″ strips to the top and bottom and then trim the ends even with the patchwork.

8 Trim your patchwork to 9″ × 9″.

Optional: Attach a piece of lightweight fusible polyester batting to the back of the patchwork.

STEP 6

STEP 8

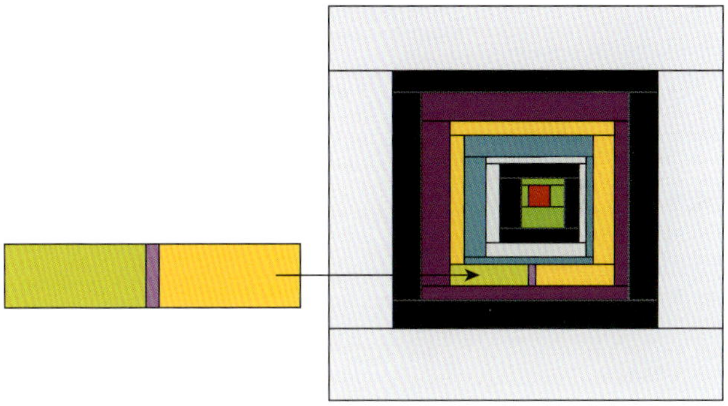

Finishing

1 For the dark gray base, cut a rectangle to the same width and add 1″ for the length. For this 9″ × 9″ patchwork, cut a 9″ × 10″ rectangle. Slice the rectangle in half lengthwise to yield 2 rectangles, 9″ × 5″.

2 Stack the rectangles right sides together (RST) and align the long edges. Pin 2½″ from each end. Sew the pieces together with a ½″ seam allowance; begin at one edge with a backstitch, sew to the pin, and backstitch. Increase your stitch length to a long basting stitch and continue stitching to the next pin. Reduce your stitch length to the previous setting, backstitch, continue sewing to the edge, and backstitch.

3 Remove the pins and press the seam open.

4 Use a pencil or pen to mark a ¾″ × ¾″ square in each corner. Then, place the base on top of the patchwork, RST. The joining seam on the base should rest in the middle. Sew around the perimeter of the pieces, backstitching just before and just after reaching each square.

5 Cut out a ¾″ square from each corner.

6 Create boxed corners by aligning the edges where the box was trimmed. Position 1 seam up and 1 down and then sew across the cut edge. Repeat on all 4 corners.

7 Carefully remove stitches in the seam line of the base where the stitches were lengthened. Turn the pincushion right side out through the opening and stuff with fiberfill to the desired fullness.

8 Carefully pour approximately ½–¾ cup of aquarium sand on top of the fiberfill. Add a little more fiberfill or a small square of scrap fabric on top to help hold the sand in and then whipstitch the opening closed.

At this point, your pincushion is finished and ready to use. If you want to add a sturdy base to the bottom to avoid accidental pin pricks, continue with the next steps.

9 Cut a lightweight square of cardboard approximately 1″ smaller than the bottom of the pincushion.

10 Cut a square of fabric approximately 1″ larger than the cardboard. Add a small amount of glue to the bottom of the cardboard and then center it glue side down on the wrong side of the fabric square. Wrap the fabric up and over the cardboard edges and glue it in place.

11 Apply glue from edge to edge on the side of the cardboard with the raw edges. The fabric-covered side will be on the bottom. Press the glued side to the bottom of the pincushion, covering the whip-stitched opening. Let the glue set overnight before using.

STEP 2

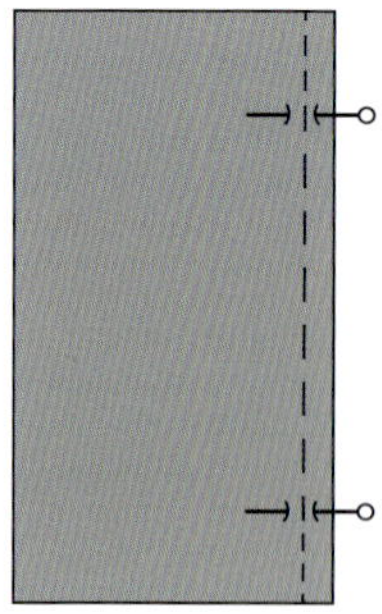

STEP 4

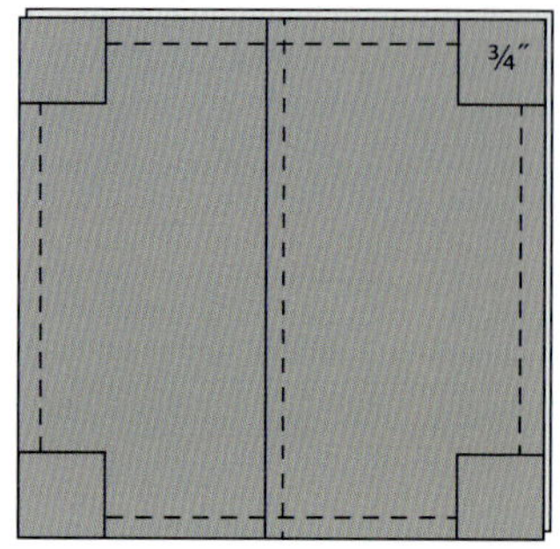

STEP 5

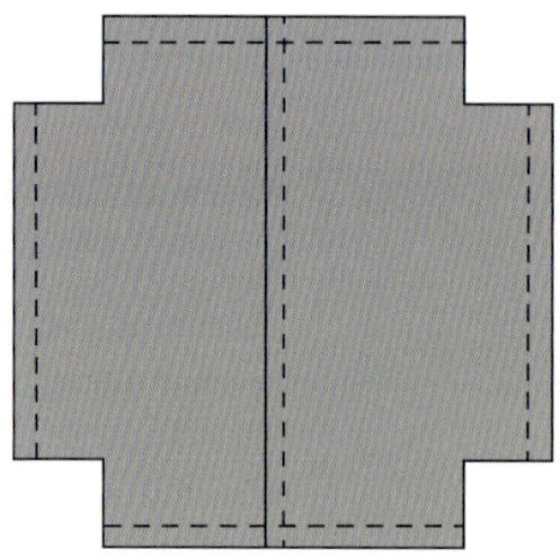

STEP 6

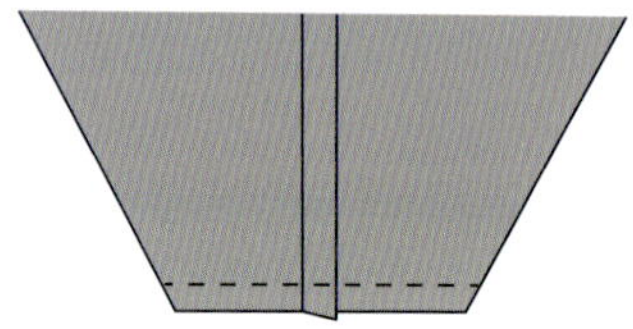

ELEVATE GREETING CARD

Finished card:: 7″ × 5″

There is nothing like a handmade card for someone special. Whip up a Little block, attach it to a blank card, and you'll send off something that won't just be saved—it's likely to be framed!

Materials

Yardages are based on 40″-wide fabric.

When using scraps, keep them close at hand and trim to size as you go. This design also looks great in solids!

Variety of light-value small-scale print scraps: 20 or more strips 1″ × 5″

Variety of bright pink and red small-scale print scraps: 20 or more strips 1″ × 5″

Bright pink small-scale print scraps: 2 strips approximately 1″ × 8″

Blank card: 5″ × 7″ or 8½″ × 11″ card stock

Glue stick

After adding each new piece, finger-press the seam away from the piece just added.

1 Sort your fabric into 2 stacks, the light values in one and the pinks and reds in another. Choose the center red/pink piece and the next 2 light fabrics for the top and bottom sections. Trim the center piece to ¾″ × ¾″ and the light pieces roughly into 1″ × 1″ squares. Sew a light piece right sides together (RST) to the top and bottom of the center square. Finger-press the seams away from the center and trim any overhanging excess fabric from the top and bottom edges.

STEP 1

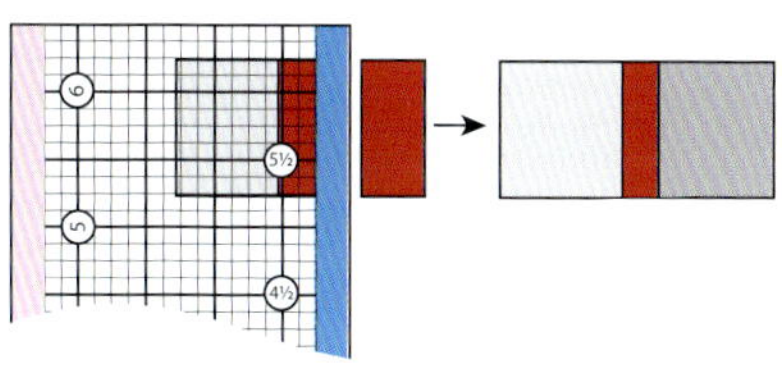

2 Choose 2 pink/red fabric strips and, with RST, sew a strip to one side and finger-press the seam away from the center. Use your Reveal Ruler to trim the opposite side of the unit to approximately ⅛″ and then add the second pink/red strip.

STEP 2

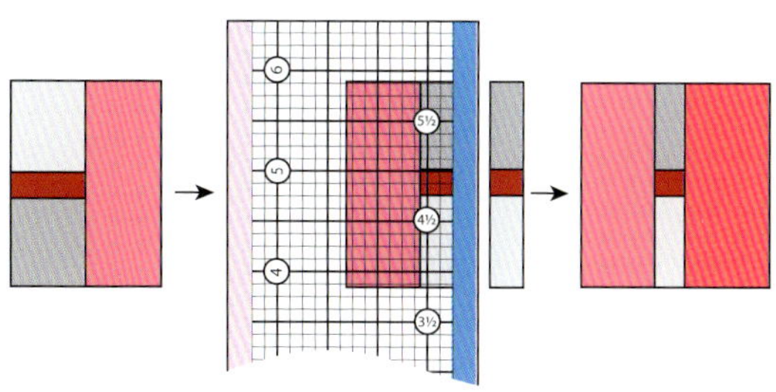

3 Use your Reveal Ruler to trim the light-value fabrics added in Step 1 to approximately ⅛″. Add the next 2 light pieces, RST, to these newly trimmed edges. Finger-press away from the center piece.

4 Continue adding pieces in this manner, repeating Steps 2 and 3, alternating between adding light and pink/red pieces. Trim these rounds to approximately ⅛″ each until you have a total of 9 rounds. *Note:* Add as many rounds as desired or increase the widths as desired.

5 Add a final round of light value and pink/red pairs and trim these last 4 pieces to approximately ½″.

6 Once the block is complete, press and trim any loose edges and threads.

7 Center the block on the front of the card and mark a dot on the card front just inside and underneath all 4 corners. Remove the block and carefully apply a line of glue from dot to dot on the card front and in an X through the center. Align the block on the card, matching the corner dots, and adhere it to the card front. *Optional:* If you are using card stock, trim your piece to 7″ × 10″ and fold in half to result in a 7″ × 5″ card.

8 For an extra bit of color, apply a line of glue along the long edges of the card. Press the longer pink strips along the top and bottom edges. Fold the top edge over to the back and secure with a line of glue. Repeat for the bottom edge of the card, splitting the width between the front and inside of the card.

STEP 3

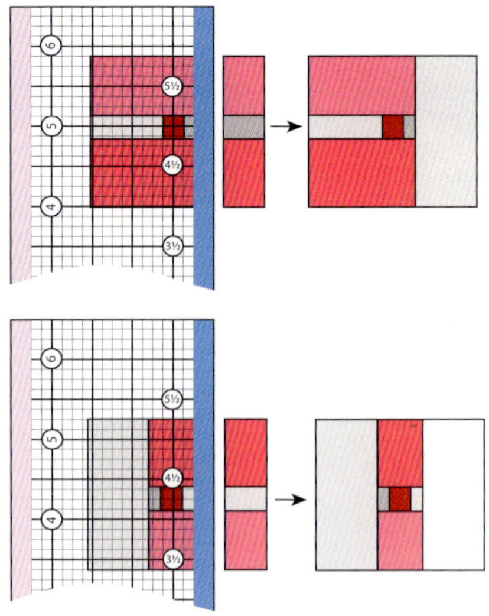

STEP 4

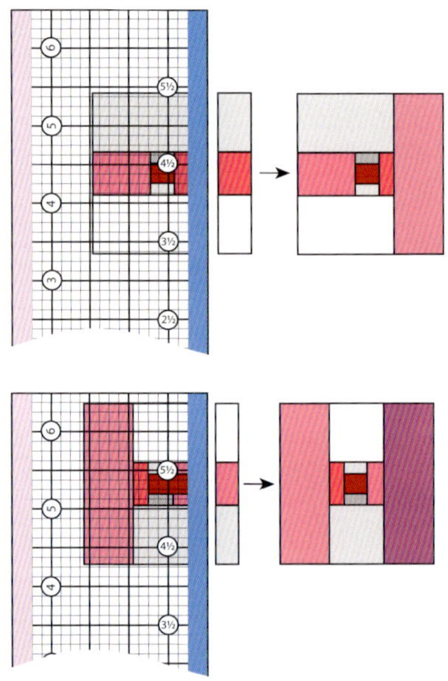

STEP 5

TRAILBLAZER PLACE MATS

Finished place mat: 16½″ × 13½″
These instructions make 4 place mats.

I love spending quality time on small projects that don't use yards and yards of fabric and result in something I can enjoy daily, wash and dry, and use over and over again without worry. These place mats fit the bill perfectly and can be sewn up over a weekend—perfect for a retreat project or as a nice gift. They provide a great opportunity to try out new piecing methods, and they are easy to quilt on a domestic machine without a lot of stress.

With this project, you get to take the training wheels off! Although I give suggested blocks for the accent, you can choose to follow my example and play. You only need to make sure that your completed block finishes at the same size as the blocks in the instructions. Enjoy!

Materials

Yardages are based on 40″-wide fabric.

If you choose to use your existing scraps or yardage, you can skip right to the cutting list to find the dimensions of the pieces you'll need.

Variety of light gray solids: 4 pieces, ½ yard each

Variety of light to dark ruby and purple solids: 12 pieces, ⅛ yard each

Variety of medium-light to dark aqua and teal solids: 7 pieces, ⅛ yard each

Variety of light to medium mint green solids: 3 pieces, ⅛ yard each

Batting: crib size

Basting spray

Cutting

Light Gray

Cut each of the gray ½-yard pieces into a 22″ × 18″ rectangle and an 18″ × 18″ square. Set aside the remaining 18″ squares for backings. Subcut the 22″ × 18″ rectangles into 3 sections each:

1 strip 1½″ × 22″

1 rectangle 14″ × 18″

1 rectangle 4½″ × 3½″

Construction

Use one of the 1½″ × 22″ gray strips in each block.

Blocks

For the blocks below, after sewing each seam, remove the combination from the sewing machine and finger-press the seam away from the center square. You can make the blocks your own by varying the widths of the logs or even angling some of them. You can also select an entirely different block—just ensure that the blocks all finish at 4½″ × 4½″.

TIP

I only trim when I'm ready to add a new piece, which allows me to make design decisions as I go. Having the ability to determine the width and design as you go is part of the fun of this method! Keep the desired finished block size in mind as you work, but don't stress if your blocks look different or have more or fewer rounds than mine.

COURTHOUSE STEPS

Begin with a center square in your desired color and size, approximately 1″ × 1″. Add pieces to the top, bottom, left, and right. Continue adding rounds in this manner for a total of 5 rounds. Use your Reveal Ruler to trim to approximately ¼″–⅜″ before adding each new piece. Leave the last round at least ½″ wide and trim the block to 4½″ × 4½″.

KEYHOLE

Begin with a center square in your desired color and size, approximately 1″ × 1″. Add a gray background piece to one side. Trim by using your Reveal Ruler and then add the first color to the same side. Rotate 90° and add 2 more pieces, trimming before you add each piece. Rotate another 90°, add 2 more pieces, and then repeat once more to complete your first round. Continue in this manner to add 2 more rounds. Always add the gray/neutral piece first and then the color for that round. Follow the color order in the photo to replicate my block or alternate colors as you wish. Leave the last round at least ½″ wide and trim the block to 4½″ × 4½″. *Note:* To fit 3 rounds in this small block, trim to ¼″–⅜″ before adding each piece. Trim even smaller if you want to add more rounds!

MODIFIED SQUARE IN A SQUARE

Begin with a center square in your desired color and size, approximately 1½″ × 1½″. Follow the instructions for Little Square in a Square (page 24). Alternate between narrow (approximately ⅛″ or less) and wide (¼″ or more) for each round. Continue adding rounds in this manner for a total of 4 gray and 4 color rounds. Leave the last round at least ½″ wide and trim the block to 4½″ × 4½″.

SPIRAL

Begin with a center square in your desired color and size, approximately 1″ × 1″. Follow the instructions for Little Spiral, Light Center (page 25). Change colors as shown in the photo or as desired. Continue adding rounds in this manner for a total of 5½ rounds. (The last half round has 2 color pieces.) Leave the last round at least ½″ wide and trim the block to 4½″ × 4½″. *Note:* To fit 5½ rounds, trim the gray background strips to approximately ¼″ and the color strips to approximately ⅜″. You can also choose different sizes and sew more or fewer rounds, keeping in mind that the block needs to finish at 4½″ × 4½″.

Making the Place Mats

1 Sew a different gray rectangle 3″ × 4½″ to the right side of each completed block. Press the seam away from the block and set aside.

2 Subcut each 18″ × 14″ rectangle into 13½″ × 14″ and 4½″ × 14″ rectangles. Pair each 4½″ piece with a 13½″ piece, making sure that each is paired with a different gray.

STEP 1

STEP 2

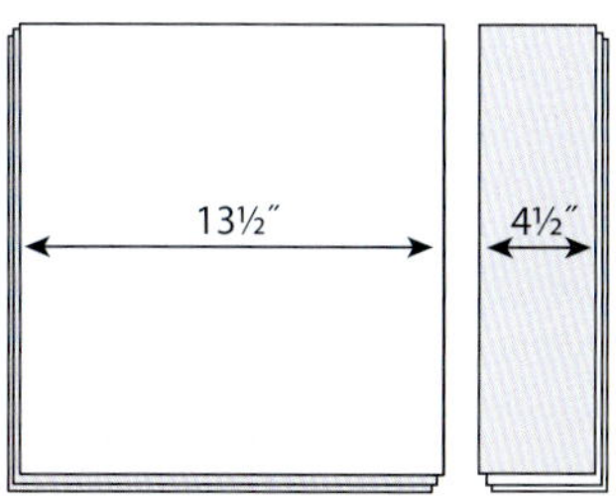

3 Cut 4 strips 1″ × 14″ of leftover block fabric for the vertical bridge. Refer to Bridges (page 28) and add a bridge combining each of the pairs from Step 2. Press the seams away from the bridge.

4 Subcut each unit made in Step 3 into an 11″ × 14″ rectangle and an approximately 6⅝″ × 14″ bridge unit. *Note:* The exact size of the smaller rectangle will depend on the width of your bridge. There will be 2¼″ between the bridge and the left edge.

5 Measure 3″–4″ down from the top edge of each bridge unit and cut horizontally. Match the gray color on the right side of the bridge with a block unit from Step 1 that has the same color added to its right side. Align the left edges and sew the 3 sections together. *Don't worry if the side piece is too wide; trim all to the same width in the steps below.*

6 Lay the bridge and block combination to the right of a gray 11″ × 14″ rectangle, matching the inside gray colors. The bridge section is longer, so you can shift it up or down until you are happy with the result. Once you're satisfied with the layout, pin and stitch the pieces together. Press the seam toward the 11″-wide piece, and trim the top, bottom, and right sides even. Repeat Steps 2–5 to complete the remaining place-mat tops.

7 Measure the finished size of your place-mat top. Select one of the backing pieces and trim it to match the size of your top. Cut a piece of batting that is ¼″ smaller than the top on all sides. Center and spray baste the batting to the backing. Center and layer the place-mat top, right sides together, with the backing. Pin around all 4 sides.

8 Sew around all 4 edges, leaving an opening for turning. If you have a walking foot or dual/even feed foot, use that to stitch the pieces together. Clip the corners, carefully turn the place mat right side out, and use the blunt end of a pair of scissors to poke the corners out, being careful not to poke a hole through the fabric. Roll the seam between your thumb and finger to flatten it out along the edge and pin it. Fold the opening shut and pin it. Lightly press all 4 edges to set the batting in the seam. Hand stitch the opening closed.

9 Quilt as desired.

Repeat Steps 6–9 to complete all four place mats.

STEP 3

STEP 4

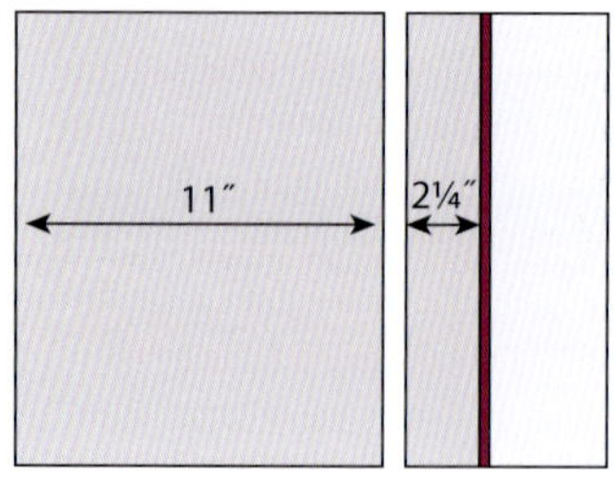

STEP 5

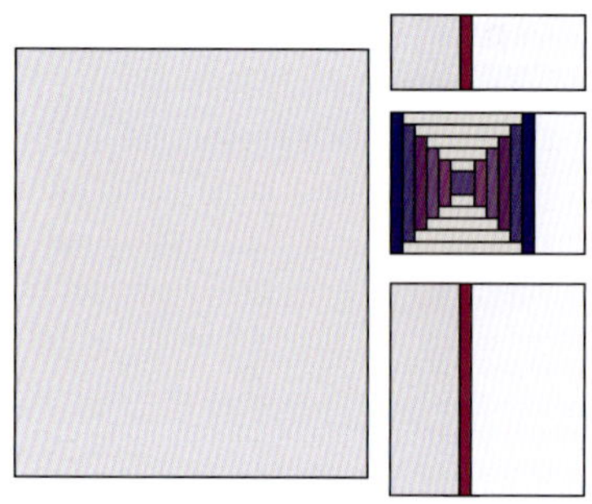

STEP 6

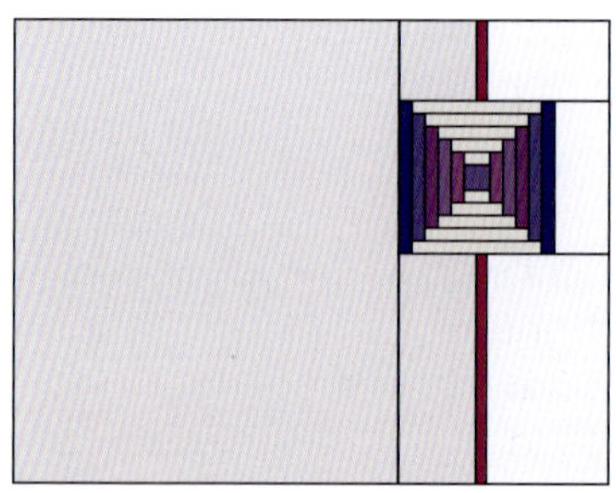

STEP 7

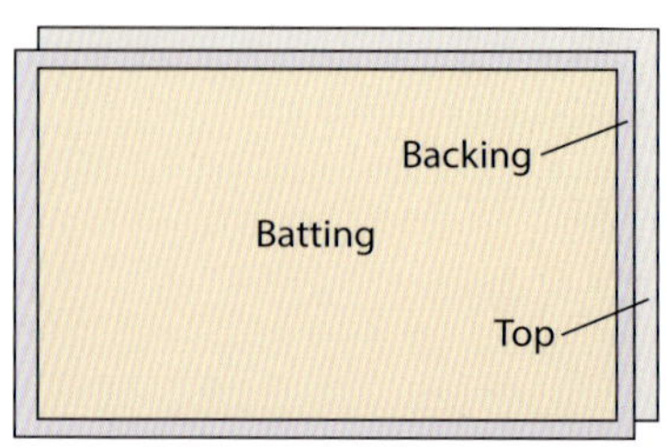

LOVE LETTERS WALL HANGING

Finished wall hanging:
approximately 12″ × 6″

Possibly the best four-letter word in the English language and the perfect project for someone you love. And because it has only four letters, it is the ideal size to practice your new letter-making skills.

Materials

Yardages are based on 40″-wide fabric.

Variety of light-value prints or solids for the background: ¼ yard or equivalent scraps

Variety of dark-value prints or solids for letters: 4 strips 2½″ × 20″

Backing: 1 rectangle 14″ × 8″

Binding: 1 strip 40″ × 2½″

Batting: 1 rectangle 14″ × 8″

Construction

Note: When you're piecing the letters, keep in mind that they don't need to be exact or perfectly straight—that is the charm of piecing the letters by using the Reveal Method!

1 Start with the letter L. Cut a letter and background fabric to approximately 3″ × 5″ and layer one atop the other. Place the ruler on top and adjust it to cut a slight vertical angle. Discard the right side of the letter fabric and the left side of the background fabric. Sew the remaining 2 pieces together to form the long part of the letter "L." Finger-press the seams to one side and set aside.

2 Estimate the desired size and cut a section of letter fabric for the bottom part of the letter "L." Cut a small piece of background fabric and sew it to the short end of the letter fabric. Use your ruler and trim the top edge as desired; set aside.

STEP 1

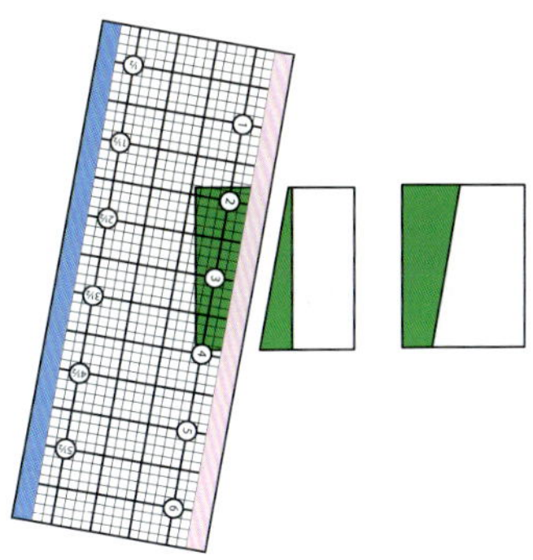

STEP 2

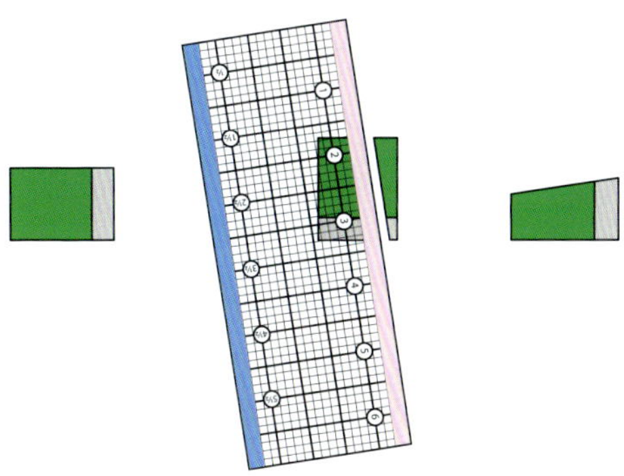

3 Match the bottom portion of the letter with the top part made in Step 1. Trim the bottom edge of the top piece to match the top angle of the bottom piece. Sew the 2 pieces together to form the letter "L." Trim a small width of background fabric to the same length as the letter "L" as sew to the left side. Add a strip of background fabric to the left side of the block and set aside.

4 Using the size of your "L" for reference, cut 2 rectangles approximately half the height of the "L" for the letter "O." Cut a background piece for the center part to the same height, but a bit wider. Sew the 3 pieces together. Eyeball the size and cut 2 additional pieces for the top and bottom of the "O." Use your Reveal Ruler to adjust and then trim off all 4 corners at different angles, as desired.

5 Cut a background-fabric square slighty smaller than the "O." Slice the square from corner to corner in both directions to create 4 triangles. Sew a triangle to each corner. Trim all edges straight or at a slight angle, as desired.

6 Refer to the size of the letter "L" and cut a background rectangle approximately the same size. Use your ruler to adjust and trim away the right and left sides to create the center portion of the letter "V." Cut 2 strips of letter fabric longer than the background. Sew 1 strip to the left side, with the top and bottom end pieces extending beyond the background edges. Trim the inside angle to match the background. Add the second piece to the right side.

STEP 3

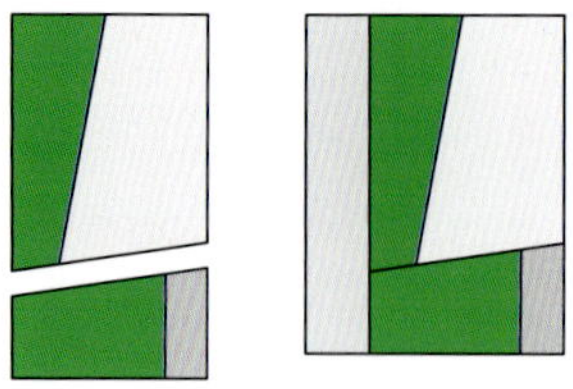

STEP 4

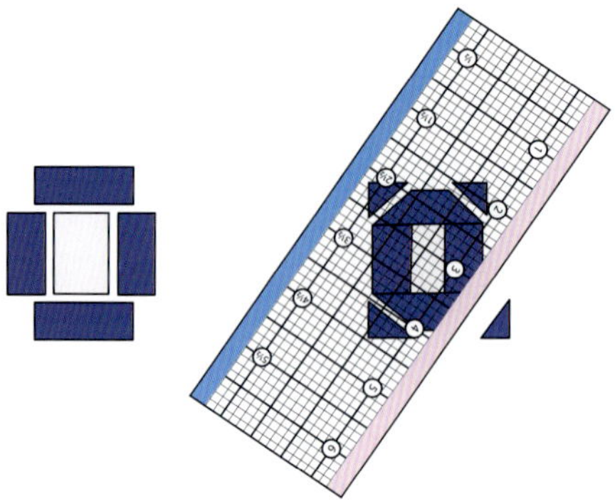

STEP 5

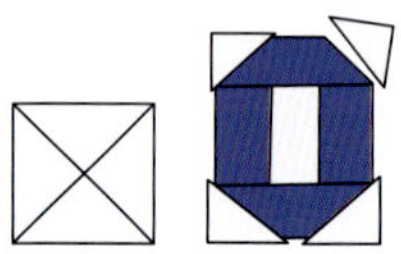

STEP 6

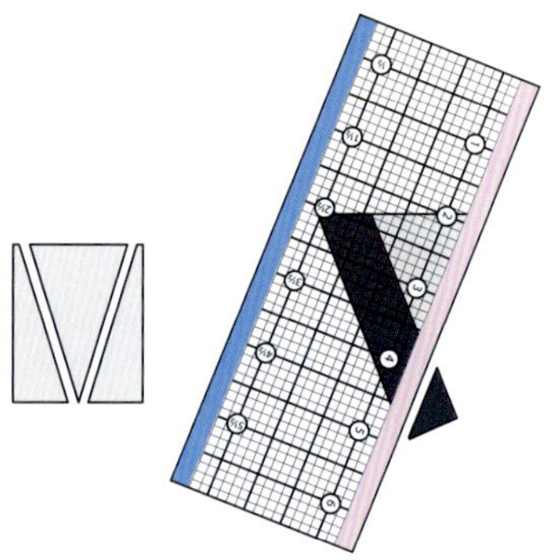

7 Cut 2 background rectangles longer than the "V" section. Trim the left piece to the same angle as the left side of the "V" and sew it in place. Trim the excess at the bottom. Repeat for the right side.

8 For the letter "E," cut 3 letter-fabric rectangles and 2 background-fabric rectangles. Layer the background pieces and 1 letter piece and use your ruler to adjust and trim an angle along both long edges. Discard the top and bottom cuts, and arrange the 3 wedge-shaped pieces as shown. Place the 2 remaining letter rectangles right sides together, match the angle along the top piece, and then cut. Arrange and sew the 5 pieces together.

9 Trim a length of letter fabric for the vertical side of the letter "E." Sew it to the left side of the unit from Step 8.

10 Combine the letter blocks, adding background sections to fill in the space at the top, bottom, and sides of the letters, as needed. Layer with batting and backing, and quilt as desired by machine or hand. Add a binding by using your favorite method.

STEP 7

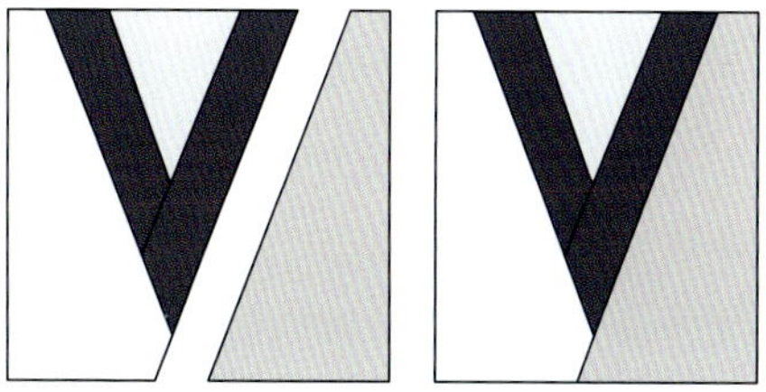

STEP 8

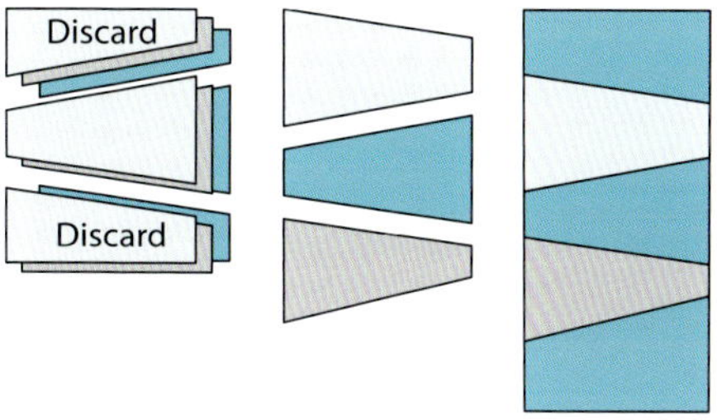

STEP 9

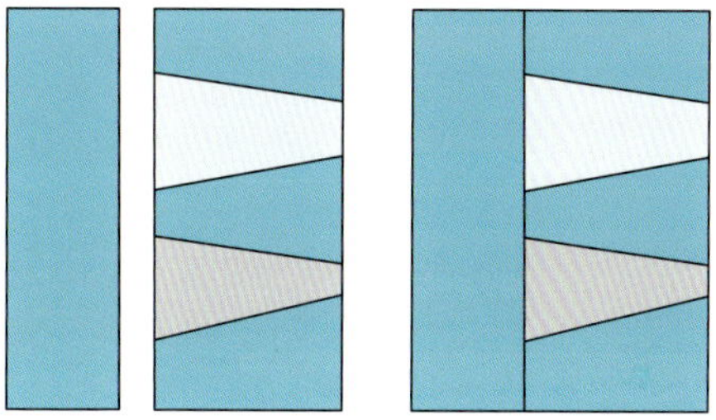

STEP 10

BOHO COASTERS

Finished coaster:
Approximately 5″ diameter

Forget fluffy mug rugs: This set of coasters is as unique as it is practical. They lay perfectly flat, so your cups won't tip, and when they get dirty, you can just pop them in the dishwasher and lay them flat to dry. Each one is different than the next—all of your friends will be begging for a set! Just don't tell them how easy they are to make.

These coasters are made by simply adding rings or rounds of different colors around a center piece or block. You can make a variety of sizes, depending on when you decide to stop adding rounds. Consider making larger versions for trivets, candle mats, or plant bases. Enjoy!

Materials

Yardages are based on 40″-wide fabric.

If you choose to use your existing scraps or yardage, you can skip right to the cutting list to find the dimensions of the pieces you'll need.

Assorted scraps:
7–10 contrasting colors for each coaster

Backing: ¼ yard or a fat quarter

Batting: 1 square 6″ × 6″

Cutting

From the scraps for the top, cut rectangles approximately 2″ × 12″. Keep them close at hand as you create your coasters.

For the backing, cut 2 squares 6″ × 7″

From the batting, cut 1 square 6″ × 6″

Construction

Finger-press the seams to one side as you add the pieces.

1 Subcut 3 different colored rectangles 1½″ × 2″ from the scraps. Sew 2 of these right sides together (RST) along the long edges and finger-press the seam to one side. Use your Reveal Ruler to trim away one edge, crossing over the seam allowance at an angle. Add the third rectangle to the other side to complete the center section.

2 Choose a new color for Round 1 to make a ring around the patchwork made in Step 1. Trim a new edge at an interesting angle, crossing over a seam when you can. Add the new color piece to the trimmed edge.

STEP 1

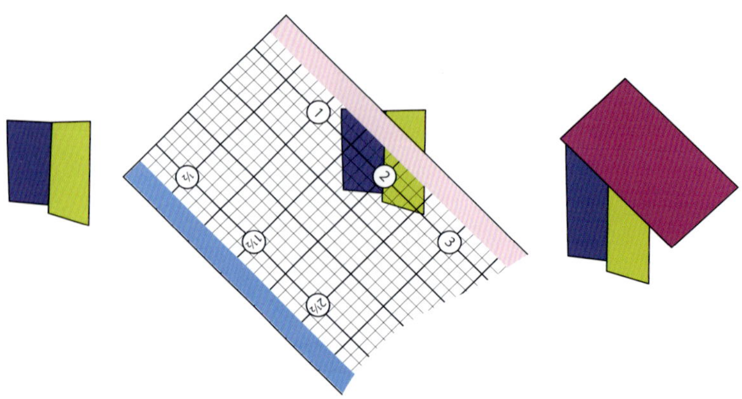

3 Move on to a new side and continue Round 1, using your ruler to view the center patchwork each time you prepare to add a new strip. Don't trim any other edges of the coaster until you are ready to add a piece to that edge, unless there's an excess end flap in the way. You can work in a clockwise or counterclockwise order. There are no rules—you can even add pieces on one side and then move to the opposite side as you use your ruler to help design the center shape. Continue to add pieces until Round 1 is complete. Leave the round untrimmed.

4 Choose a new color for Round 2. Use your ruler to trim off an edge of Round 1 at an interesting angle, crossing over a seam when you can. Add the new Round 2 piece to the trimmed edge. Repeat Step 3 with the Round 2 color until the round is complete.

5 Continue adding rounds in this manner, with each round being a new contrasting color. Try to trim each piece differently from one to the next. Add pieces until you reach the size you'd like. My ideal size for mug coasters is 4″–5″ in diameter. Make sure that the last round is wide enough to include a ¼″ seam allowance to turn the edges under.

6 Once the top of your coaster is complete, trim a piece of thin batting to the final shape you'd like your coaster to be with 5 or more sides and set it aside. Cut 2 rectangles for the backing, both sized 2″ taller and 1″ wider than the coaster. For a roughly 5″ diameter coaster, the backing rectangles can be 6″ × 7″

TIP

In the interests of using up your leftovers, if you have thick batting scraps you can separate it into thinner layers as desired.

7 Sew the long edges together and press the seam open.

8 Layer the backing RST with the coaster. Place the batting piece on top and pin the 3 layers together.

9 Sew all the way around the perimeter of the batting and backstitch. Trim the edges to ¼″.

STEP 3

STEP 4

STEP 5

STEP 7

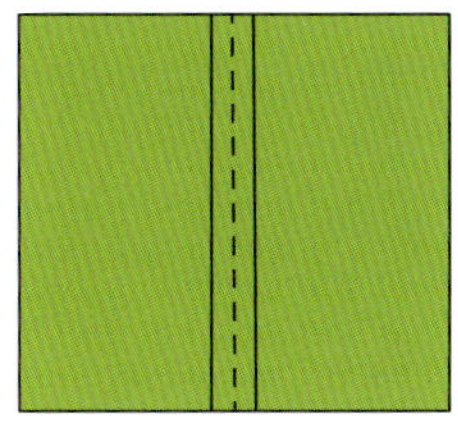

STEP 8

STEP 10

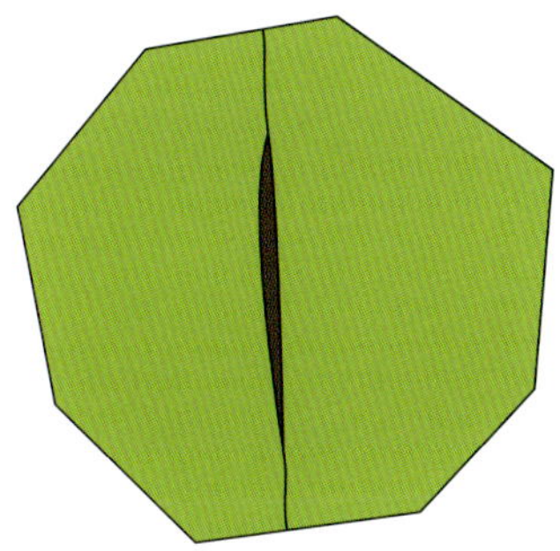

10 Using a seam ripper, carefully remove about 2″ of the center backing seam. Turn the coaster right side out, using a pointy object to push out any corners. Press flat with an iron. Whipstitch the opening closed.

11 Have fun and machine quilt the coaster as desired!

ABOUT THE AUTHOR

In 1994, Karla, her husband, two sons, and their dog moved to Kodiak Island, Alaska. The dark, nearly sunless days seemed endless. With a two-year-old in tow and no family around, Karla emptied boxes one by one as they arrived. It was a nice surprise when she opened a box and rediscovered a quilt her mom had made for her when she was a teenager. She'd always loved the quilt, and even in its torn and tattered condition, she realized it was the next best thing to a hug! She wrapped herself up in it, and it was right then that she decided to make a quilt herself.

Rediscovering this quilt started her on a quilting journey. At the Kodiak library, the only two quilt books she found interesting were on paper piecing and art quilts. Surprisingly, Karla found harmony between the two of them and ended up enjoying both styles. Once she figured out the paper-piecing methods, she was amazed and immediately began redrafting blocks smaller and smaller. She studied the art quilt book, taking in tips on color and piecing. It was an unlikely mix, but it established her style. Before long, she was making teeny-tiny blocks and sneaking them into larger improv quilts. At the time, improv art quilts weren't mainstream, but she'd found her niche and hasn't stopped to this day.

After three years on Kodiak Island, her family moved to Salem, Oregon, where she discovered Mid-Valley Quilt Guild and her soon to be favorite quilt shop, Greenbaums Quilted Forest. In no time at all, her quilting life took over. It all happened rather quickly, with ideas continuing to bubble up. After writing eight quilt books, she still designs in her dreams, does math as she drives, is inspired by colors from the forest to the coast, and sketches tiled floors into quilt blocks!

Visit Karla online and follow on social media!

Website: saginawstreetquilts.com

Instagram: @karlaquilts

Facebook: /saginawstreetquilts

YouTube: /karlaalexander9006